"I knew Brother Roger personally for a long time, and I had a relationship of warm friendship with him. He had often visited me, and, as I said in Rome, the day of his death I had received a letter from him that went directly to my heart. . . . I think that we should listen to him, listen from within to the ecumenism that he lived out spiritually, and allow ourselves to he led by his witness towards an ecumenism that is truly inward and spiritual."

—POPE BENEDICT XVI

"Very few people in a generation manage to change the whole climate of a religious culture; but Brother Roger did just this. . . . He changed the image of Christianity itself for countless young people. . . . His authority was authentically monastic—the authority of a father and elder brother in God who drew his vision from patient waiting on the Lord in prayer, and from the work and study and discernment of a committed community."

—ROWAN WILLIAMS
Former Archbishop of Canterbury

"The vision of peace and reconciliation in 'God's today' which guided Brother Roger's commitment and that of the community he founded has been a source of inspiration and spiritual renewal for generations of young people, in Europe and throughout the world. Under his spiritual leadership, the Taizé Community has offered a model of how the praise of God is integrally linked to solidarity with the least fortunate. For many of us, Brother Roger incarnated the hope that the Christian faith can bring to the world."

—GENEVIÈVE JACQUES
Former Secretary General, World Council of Churches, Switzerland

"Brother Roger was known throughout the whole world. Man of inspired words, man of prayer, zealous worker in the fields of Christ—his untiring search to establish relationships of peace and love among Christians and his commitment to transmitting the Christian ideal to the youth of Europe earned him universal respect."

—ALEXY II (1929–2008)
First Patriarch of Moscow and All Russia in the post-Soviet period

"When I came in mission to Estonia after the terrible years of communism, I understood what Brother Roger meant by the 'power of the provisional,' which leaves all the room to God and God alone. I shall ever be grateful to him for that. . . . He was called Roger and his name, everywhere it was pronounced, sang the consoling tenderness and freshness of God for all who were in pain and suffering."

—METROPOLITAN STEPHANOS OF TALLIN
Primate of the Orthodox Church of Estonia

"Brother Roger came twice to Dresden for a prayer with young people and he stayed at my home. The Kreuzkirche was filled to overflowing, and other churches too. It was a profound moment of hope for many young people, right in the midst of the era of the German Democratic Republic. His spiritual openness to the will of God and God's commandments also remains unforgettable. . . . What a life in the footsteps of Christ!"

—JOHANNES HEMPEL (1929–2020)
Lutheran Bishop of Dresden during the time of Communism

"Brother Roger was a good friend and brother to our Mother, Mother Teresa; to our late Holy Father, Pope John Paul II; to the young; and to all regardless of religion, race, nationality, or social status. He has left behind thousands of friends on earth and will surely be welcomed by a host of friends in heaven."

—SISTER M. NIRMALA (1924–2015)
Successor to Mother Teresa as Superior General, Missionaries of Charity,
Kolkata, India

"For me, Brother Roger was one of the spiritual pillars of Europe in its movement towards unity."

—VACLAV HAVEL (1936–2011)
Former President of the Czech Republic

"Following the finest traditions of the faith that sustained him, Brother Roger consecrated his life to the service of peace, dialogue, and reconciliation. He became the untiring advocate of the values of respect, of tolerance, and of solidarity, in particular toward the young. His message of hope and of trust will remain a source of inspiration for all."

—KOFI ANNAN (1938–2018)
Former Secretary General of the United Nations

The Journals
of Brother Roger *of* Taizé

The Journals
of BROTHER ROGER
of TAIZÉ

Volume 1: 1941–1968

 CASCADE *Books* · Eugene, Oregon

THE JOURNALS OF BROTHER ROGER OF TAIZÉ
Volume 1: 1941–1968

Cascade Books
An Imprint of Wipf and Stock Publishers
199 W. 8th Ave., Suite 3
Eugene, OR 97401

www.wipfandstock.com

PAPERBACK ISBN: 978-1-7252-9792-0
HARDCOVER ISBN: 978-1-7252-9793-7
EBOOK ISBN: 978-1-7252-9794-4

Cataloguing-in-Publication data:

Names: Brother Roger of Taizé.

Title: The journals of Brother Roger of Taizé : volume 1: 1941–1968 / Brother Roger of Taizé.

Description: Eugene, OR: Cascade Books, 2021 | Includes bibliographical references and index.

Identifiers: ISBN 978-1-7252-9792-0 (paperback) | ISBN 978-1-7252-9793-7 (hardcover) | ISBN 978-1-7252-9794-4 (ebook)

Subjects: LCSH: Roger, frère, 1915–2005—Diaries | Christian Life | Spirituality | Communauté de Taizé

Classification: BX9459.S38 R64 2021 (paperback) | BX9459.S38 (ebook)

10/19/21

Translation, notes, and commentaries by the Taizé Community.

Contents

Introduction

For many people in the English-speaking world, the name "Taizé" evokes a kind of short repetitive chant used in the context of a meditative worship service, or perhaps even more the style of prayer in which such chants are employed. Others know Taizé as a place in rural France where tens of thousands of young Christians flock each year to spend a week of prayer and reflection in the context of a community life.

What is not always understood, however, is the underlying reality that makes possible both the worship and the gatherings of young people. A tiny village in eastern France, since 1940 Taizé has been the site of an ecumenical community of brothers rooted in the monastic tradition. Today it is made up of around a hundred brothers, from over 25 different countries and from different Christian traditions, Reformed, Lutheran, Anglican, and Catholic, who commit themselves for life to an existence made up of common prayer, work to earn their living, and hospitality. They strive to live as a "parable of community," a sign of unity in the midst of divided Christians.

The Taizé Community began thanks to one man, known as Brother Roger, born on May 12, 1915 in French-speaking Switzerland. His father, Charles Schutz, was a pastor in the Swiss Reformed Church, and his mother, Amélie Marsauche, came from a family whose roots were in France. The youngest of nine children, seven girls and two boys, Roger felt called to be a writer from an early age. Following his return to the faith after an adolescent religious crisis and a long bout with tuberculosis that brought him close to death, he decided to study theology, more in accordance with his father's wishes than out of a desire to become the pastor of a congregation.

As a young man, Roger was deeply concerned about the growing individualism in society that was leaving its mark on the church as well. In addition, he was convinced that transmitting the message of Jesus Christ by words alone was not enough. Although in Europe everyone by now was familiar with the figure of Jesus and his teaching, this knowledge seemingly no longer had the power to move mountains. What was needed, according to Roger, were concrete signs that would manifest the truth and beauty of the gospel. This led him to examine the age-old tradition of intentional community life in the Christian church and its possible relevance for our time.

When the Second World War broke out and the north of France was occupied by the Nazi armies, Roger felt called to leave neutral Switzerland and settle in France. He wanted to be close to the victims of the war, as well as continuing to reflect on the creation of a community. In August 1940 he found an abandoned house for sale in the small, isolated hamlet of Taizé, in Burgundy, and purchased it. After the war, Taizé became the home of the community which Brother Roger founded and of which he served as prior until his tragic death on August 16, 2005 at the hand of a demented person, during evening prayer in the church.

Throughout his life, the founder of Taizé was in the habit of jotting down thoughts and reflecting on daily events in notebooks used for that purpose or, especially in his later years, on small bits of paper. These writings helped him to reflect on essential aspects of his existence; they were part of an attempt to forge what he called "the unity of the personality." This unity, however, was never just an individualistic endeavor for him. As a Christian, Brother Roger felt it was essential to discover the salient traits of the age in which he lived, in order to discover how to be present in the contemporary world as a follower of Christ. Moreover, it was often through personal encounters that he was able better to understand his own identity and the society around him.

This book contains the journals of Brother Roger. In some cases they are fragmentary in nature, often because the originals were lost or destroyed. Beginning in 1972, however, Brother Roger began publishing his diaries, interspersed with short meditations. Six volumes saw the light of day, covering the years from 1969 to 1981. These collected insights, reflections and accounts of personal encounters and current events offer what is perhaps the best portrait of the founder of Taizé. Moreover, they bring to light key aspects of the community that continues to attempt to put into practice the vision that inspired him.

The Early Years

Brother Roger, in his mid-twenties, spent the years from 1940 to 1942 in Taizé. With his sister Genevieve, he offered shelter to refugees, mainly Jews, fleeing the Nazi persecution. In 1942, while he was away in Switzerland, the police broke into his house and, warned in time, he did not return. In Geneva he met the young men who would become his first three brothers.

April 23, 1941

Met this morning on the way to Massilly[1] a worker returning from catching fish. A windfall: he hopes to have some fish to sell in the coming days. We talk about the present situation. He is unable to feed his family. I gather from his words that he has been a militant in the Communist party. I try to understand. He promises to sell me some fish. I point out my house in the distance. All at once his expression changes. He takes me for the new lord of the manor. He is afraid he has spoken too openly and the look of distress on his face haunts me.

April 24, 1941

Awake at dawn, I wanted to take a walk in order to calm the heartache caused by yesterday's meeting. A poor man opened his heart and immediately he was frozen by fear of the bourgeois. He is right to fear, for at this moment people like me are in charge of things.

For my own peace and quiet, the current situation is likely to last. But as a Christian, can I think of my own happiness when it is to the detriment of the weak? I know that the coming of a socialist society would cause me to be deprived of certain things.

From now on I will live in solidarity with the lowly of the earth. May this not inspire in me any hatred of the powerful.

I have made my choice. It is a costly one.

May 1941

Yesterday I went on horseback to Macon, a round-trip of seventy kilometers. The horse is so unmanageable that I wrote my will the previous evening. Coming face-to-face with the reality of death did not impress me. I could have refused to run any kind of risk whatsoever, but the thought never even crossed my mind.

---

1. A small village close to Taizé, in the direction of Cluny and Macon.

May 1941

Welcomed this morning two Jews, who arrived like a pair of hunted animals. I did not ask them for their papers and I did not try to learn their real names. Both of them have a sad history. They even gave the impression they were overstating their case, as if their actual suffering was not enough to awaken sympathy. I didn't feel that their exaggeration was a lie. Having drunk the cup to the dregs, they are not yet able to discern the limits of their distress. This phenomenon is widespread in people who have suddenly been struck by misfortune.

June 1941

We are short of food; we eat nettle soup. If the bakery in Cormatin[2] was not so understanding, we would go hungry.

Every morning I work on a text on spiritual retreat.[3] Setting apart a few days to be alone, face to face with the Lord, animates our inner silence.

Still thinking about the need for a community of men. I know well that, in spite of all my reluctance to devote my life to this, I will have to undertake it. I have spent so much time trying to thwart God's plan. I would prefer the beaten paths, fearful as I am of the bitter struggles involved.

July 1941

Fathers Couturier and Villain came to see me yesterday.[4] In their presence I felt the positive effects of the discipline I imposed on myself during my teenage years as an unbeliever. At that time I was unable to believe, but I respected the mystery of the faith,

2. A village four kilometers from Taizé in the direction of Chalon-sur-Saone.

3. Published in October 1941 with the title *Notes explicatifs.*

4. Paul Couturier (1881–1953), a Catholic priest from Lyon, was a pioneer in the ecumenical movement. He started the week of prayer for Christian unity (January 18–25) in France. Brother Roger visited him in Lyon in late 1940.

incarnated in Christians of whatever confession. I believed in the good faith of those who maintained that they experienced communion with a God who was foreign to me. That readiness to be attentive is now of service to me. I believe that today I was able to grasp from within the Roman Catholic position of those priests.

Both of them understood my concern: the indifference of Christians at our divisions. Since the Great Schism of the East and the Reformation, Christians have become used to living apart, thinking they could profess a religion of love notwithstanding. The hypocrisy is so great that we have become blind: we speak of love as the very basis of our ethics and yet we cannot stand one another. We are suspicious of one another despite the fact that we bear the same name—the name of Christ, of Christians.

In my thirst for authenticity, the scandal of division kept me captive and far from the faith; how could someone bear the name Christian, of a God of love, and accept having to choose a church, in other words to take sides against other Christians?

Our complacency in thinking that the present situation of divided Christians is normal will lead us to ruin.

Summer 1941

Read the life of Charles de Foucauld, by René Bazin.[5] How thrilling it is to read about Christ's victory over a man of great sensitivity, born to be an aesthete. At the root of everything: going to confession, followed by the obligation to take communion with no delay.

I remain confounded by his failures. Though I am clear-sighted enough to see how different my situation is from his, his failure is a salutary warning for me. It burns me within. I love life; all the education I received as a child has inclined me to joy. And

5. Charles de Foucauld (1858–1916), a French army officer and explorer, became a Catholic priest and hermit in the Sahara Desert after a radical conversion experience. He dreamed of starting a community, but died alone, assassinated by a group of bandits. Today several religious communities and associations follow his inspiration, notably the Little Sisters and Little Brothers of Jesus.

yet a vocation of combat lies before me, with the possibility of failure at the end.

Lord, remind me of your death on the cross, your failure, so that I do not stray far from you.

Re-read the Acts of the Apostles. More than ever I am sure of one thing: communities were the living stones of the Church, whether in Jerusalem, where the Gospel was lived out to its most extreme consequence, Christian communism; or the communities founded by Paul, bringing together families in autonomous cells, the archetype of parish communities.

October 22, 1944

Again I take up this journal, abandoned since I was forced to leave Taizé. November 11, 1942–October 22, 1944. I arrived this evening with Max and Pierre.[6] It is hard for us to celebrate, since we cannot easily forget the departed whom we will never see again.

No journals survive for the years from 1944 to 1948. After the war, the small group of brothers settled in Taizé and began to live in community. The postwar years were not easy, since the war had left so much devastation in its wake. The brothers took in twenty young boys, orphaned by the war, raising them with the help of Brother Roger's sister Genevieve. At Easter 1949, the first seven brothers made a life-commitment to community of goods, celibacy, and accepting the orientations of the community. Brother Roger was chosen prior, a charge he occupied for the rest of his life.

6. Max Thurian (1921–1996), a theology student, and Pierre Souvairan (1921–1998), an agriculture student at the Polytechnic Institute of Zurich, met Brother Roger in Geneva during the war. Attracted by his project of community life, they lived together with him in an apartment near the Geneva cathedral, and returned with him to Taizé to become the first brothers of the nascent community.

September 10, 1948

Our friend L. has just spent two days with us. I am struck by his unaffected disposition, his subtlety, his nuanced judgment. I appreciate his search for a Christian aesthetic in the service of love.

I am more convinced than ever that Christian artists have an incomparable fullness of expression at their disposal. Their love for all creatures and their striving to acquire a catholic spirit give them resources for a creation along classical lines. Not that they refuse to innovate, to be revolutionary, to become relevant, but classical in the sense that the expression of their thought does not go beyond the thought itself. Their self-effacement in order to make possible a universal comprehension of events and persons makes what they create accessible.

During our conversations, I brought up the subject of frequent communion. I was appalled that a friend, someone who knows us so well, is unaware of the meaning and the significance of the sacrament of the Lord's Supper in our community.[7]

Even if, for several weeks, it happens that I receive communion with a manifest insensibility, this does not worry me at all, since I know that Christ is really present. The Lord does not need my feelings to nourish me with the bread of life.

This infinite peace, despite the heart's indifference, is a sign for me of Christ's sovereign presence in the Eucharist.

I call to mind my whole inner journey regarding communion. Disbelieving, I saw no need at all for the Lord's Supper, since my (Calvinist) church assured me only of a spiritual presence in the Eucharist. Of what use is the Sacrament, I wondered, because when two or three gather in the name of Christ, that spiritual presence is already granted.

I am overjoyed to know today that I am the bearer of Christ in his fullness, assured of his real presence, even when no perceptible resonance attests it to human beings.

---

7. This is a clear indication that a reflection on the deeper meaning of the Eucharist began long before the entry of Catholic brothers into the community in the late 1960s. The same is true for confession: see below, journal entry for September 1, p. 12–13.

September 11, 1948

Sixty-eight years ago today, in the Jura Mountains, at Chateau des Monts,[8] my revered mother was born. I am aware of the privilege of being born of that woman always true to form, so serene in her faith and yet so lively, with such artistic talents.

October 4, 1948

For almost a month now I have abandoned this journal. Travels abroad. Many material questions and perhaps above all "the tragic sentiment of life,"[9] that inner drama that takes hold of one's whole being and keeps it captive to such an extent that written expression becomes impossible.

Last night, my brothers and I sung the night office. We did not want to begin any other way this day when part of the Church commemorates one of its most authentic witnesses: Saint Francis.[10]

October 1948

I have always found the pivot of every inner discipline in constantly putting in their place the questions that assail me: lining up the problems, deferring this or that reflection to the appropriate time, exercising control over the mind so as not to be overwhelmed by the deluge of all kinds of worries and, to this end, jotting down particular suggestions in order to deal with them later on, when the mind is rested.

---

8. A lovely house in the town of Locle, in the Swiss Jura Mountains, where the family was on holiday at that time.

9. The title of an essay written in 1912 by the Spanish philosopher Miguel de Unamuno. Brother Roger was familiar with it from seeing it on his grandmother's bedside table at the end of her life.

10. The example of Francis of Assisi was very important for the nascent community. Many years later, a small community of Franciscan friars lived in Taizé alongside the brothers.

I know well that heartaches inevitably remain. They risk overturning the entire construction when we are no longer in control of ourselves. That evil cannot be mastered by will-power; the will loses its footing there and, if it unfortunately manages to go beyond itself, it hardens what it touches in the emotional life. The spirit of mercy, of forgiveness, alone can assure an inner self-control.

October 1948

One of our brothers, whom we thought had recovered, has just suffered a relapse. The suffering that torments him keeps on welling up in me.

For the last few days I have been trying to figure out the cause of our common suffering. I try to remember what I learned about it.

Suffering is the state that we feel most strongly. Pain, by causing me to turn towards myself, absorbs the whole of my being. In it I disappear.

I then perceive in myself an almost unrecognized being that gains in inner depth what it may lose in spontaneity.

The cause is not as important as the use I make of my affliction. Revolt, resignation, self-pity . . . I want none of that bitter fruit. Merely tasting it demeans me. If I am not careful, that fruit secretes a bitter gall in my soul. I want suffering to activate a resolve in me; I want it to focus my dispersed energies, to cause me to look within, to lead me to acceptance.

Distress, whatever form you may take, I say yes to you in advance. Through the suffering imposed upon me, I want to try and go beyond myself. I know that my consenting will not spontaneously be cheerful, but why not head towards the joy of gratefulness?

October 1948

Since yesterday I have not been able to get out of my mind the conversation I had with Father X. In monastic communities he recognizes a generation gap.

Those who came before him, some of whom may still be young, are motivated by an ideal of mystical communion with Christ. To attain this, it is necessary to break with all forms of human affection, even the most noble ones. Naturally this does not mean forgetting human misery, but rather including it in one's prayer. In a life alone with God, communion with him is sufficient; human contacts only weaken it.

The younger generation answers: that is true in part, but every communion with God is manifested in the love we show for human beings. In that way we can judge whether we belong to God. For this generation, the road to communion with God also includes humanity.

The following entries cannot be dated with certainty. The first seems to be from 1948, since it mentions the night prayer the brothers celebrated daily that year. The others were most probably written between 1949 and 1953.

July (1948?)

The silence of this night is hard for me. A letter I received from L. this morning keeps going through my mind. When I first read it, it made no particular impression on me. So much other correspondence drowned it out. But the quiet of the sleeping house has brought it back to mind.

For L., I have come here with others as a way of running away from the world, taking the easy way out, irresistibly attracted by the secluded countryside and its incomparable beauty. According to him, we are no longer in the world. What is the use of our living a Christian life?

Should I reply? L. only spent a few hours with us. We were overjoyed to see him. He admired every detail, the tiny courtyard freshly covered with grass that one of us created in his spare time, transporting fifty wheelbarrows of earth. He told me that he valued that courage with no ulterior motives.

The avenue of maples and lime-trees seemed to him more attractive than anywhere else, so we set up the dinner table there.

Should I reply? I know in advance that it is a waste of time. I have to take into account emotional reactions, so hard to fathom. So many times already I have wasted time trying to explain our vocation. When it is a matter of countering one of the arguments that have been ingrained for generations, far better to throw in the towel. If only I found in L. the open mind of a man whose emotions were governed by faith, I would dare to start the debate.

I wish L. had seen us in the midst of undescribable material difficulties. Twenty boys to take care of. Constant comings and goings, friends from all the Christian confessions, people of all backgrounds.

Although we were unprepared for this, we had to do the laundry and take care of all the questions involved in housekeeping, all this for years with no running water.[11] And then, for the future, counting only on the material resources ensured by our work in common from day to day, with the determination not to accept any donations for ourselves.

The tensions involved in becoming a part of rural life are constantly present.

My conclusion: if I wanted to leave the world, I would go to the city.

But what is the use of writing to him and answering with facts? I would first of all have to open his mind to all the various spiritual realities that a non-sectarian Christian should understand. Would

11. For several years, every morning the brothers had to spend two hours bringing 300 liters of water up to the community from the well located at the bottom of the hill. The water was loaded on a cart pulled by a pair of oxen. Clothes had to be washed in the village wash-house. In 1948, the community was able to dig a well close by and install an electric pump to provide running water. In the other houses in the village, running water came only in 1952.

I manage to do this when I am familiar with the atmosphere in which he spent his youth?

When I think about the closed-mindedness of so many believers, I start to long for a church that is truly catholic, in which different currents of thought are expressed without excluding one another.

Writing down my thoughts calms me. In six hours, I will see my brothers at night prayer. The mere thought of that fortifies my heart and the solitude of my room becomes appealing.

Undated

The day after tomorrow a new brother will arrive. He is leaving his family and I know how painful it is for them to see him depart. I suffer for all of them and I would like to share their distress and tell them: instead of seeing the departure of their son as an amputation, from now on they will be enriched with new sons. This unintentional suffering we cause weighs upon me. Why does the vow to enter the supernatural order of a vocation upset Christian parents so much?

Undated

Do you remember that bicycle trip lasting several days, the fervor of your prayer at each church discovered along the road? You were opening yourself to God's call; we thought about it with great seriousness. The look on your face set your entire being on fire to such an extent that I let myself be convinced by your burning conviction, by the tone of your voice, and I agreed that you should give up the study of law for theology. And today you are in the ministry of the church.

Undated

Overcome by fatigue. Unable to pray. I let myself be borne along by the community prayer without supporting it. I offer the Lord the presence of my body. I used to detest this sluggishness I saw in so many other Christians. I would find perfect joy in being open. I know this, but I do not want it. I am waiting for the event that will strengthen my resolve. For the moment it is enough to say: Have mercy, Lord!

The event I was calling for yesterday closely followed my longing.

One of the youngest of our adopted children disobeyed Genevieve, who told me about it. Returning home, he questioned his mother. When he learned that she had spoken to me about him, he burst into tears.

To scold him, however great his wrongdoing was, is out of the question then. His mother was unable to do anything to comfort him. I had to take him in my arms and walk a good distance in order to calm his distress. . . .

A fear of punishment in this youngster who had never been disciplined. I believe in God's mercy more than his wrath, and yet would I refuse to live out forgiveness!

September 1, 19??

I was able to place my work table on the terrace. My feet sink into a lawn that the rain these days has favored.

Through the tall trees in the garden I have a commanding view of the landscape, and my eyes cannot keep from rejoicing at the mists of the earth that harmonize with the lushness of the clouds. These first signs of autumn touch me deeply.

In the furthest corner of the courtyard, in the loft of the barn, hammers are pounding at a rapid rate. The carpenters are finishing a floor so that the grain harvest can be stored.

From the bottom of the hill arises a buzzing that gets lost in the intrepid ivy above my head running all the way up to the top of the wall. I rejoice in these harmonies. My whole being is jubilant. Then I remember the darkness that overcame me yesterday.

And confession has put back into their rightful place all vain cares; I breathe freely, unburdened. Absolution restored to me the joy of forgiveness. But how hard it is to give up my Huguenot pride that taught me that true confession is only to God, with no human presence.

I believe in the value of transparency. After each confession, I realize that there is a great difference between transparency before another person and that expressed to the Lord of heaven and earth in the presence of another.

Undated

Spent the evening talking about ecumenism. We are alarmed at how easy it is for many people to see ecumenism as a way to support a Christian crusade against Marxism. To accord such a motivation to the rediscovery of unity among Christians, which would set them in opposition to other people, is unspeakable.

What then would catholic charity mean, universal love for all people on earth?

Among the Christian virtues love is the greatest of all; faith is nothing without it. Had I faith enough to move mountains, or were I to give my body to the flames, if I have no charity, the love of the living Christ, I am nothing.[12]

How can we be surprised at our inability to reach the masses when we offer this hideous face of divisions among Christians, and between Christians and those who are opposed to our faith?

Should we be astonished at the impossibilities in which we find ourselves, and even at the preconceived notions people have concerning Christianity today, when we do not profess charity at all times and for all people without discrimination?

12. See 1 Cor 13:2–3.

1953–1955

By the 1950s the community had achieved a certain stability. And yet, reading between the lines of these journal entries, it is clear that difficulties and tensions never completely ceased—financial worries, crises in the lives of brothers and the suffering of friends, the state of the divided churches and of the world. But in the midst of sometimes dramatic moments, the founder of Taizé was constantly driven by the passionate search to root his life in the joy of Christ and the Gospel, to focus on signs of hope and be grateful for them.

December 1953

At the beginning of winter the countryside becomes distasteful to me. I don't like the death of the trees and the fields. The absence of life in the village weighs upon me. I dream about the times when we lived together in town. Attracted to the department stores as evening falls, the streets alive with people, the light, the overflowing life. There is no way out but to stop making comparisons.

Recall our vocation to praise. Look for new values in the intimacy and the serene peace of the house. Love solitude. Profit from this time of year to become perfectly oneself.

Try as I may to repeat to myself these objective reasons for my inner life, a regret still looms—a longing for that intimate Switzerland in wintertime. I think this is the only time of year when I miss it.

In the city, there is an announcement of Christmas that appears in the shop windows. Here, we have to discover the announcement of the Son of God in this land of fields and woods. We are in Bethlehem with the shepherds, not in Jerusalem. We have to discover it in the stables and the houses of the poor. In the silence we have to listen to the sighing of nature, and Christmas will burst forth in triumph.

Be attentive to the liturgy. Upon awakening cry out to God my joy for this Advent day, for this sacred waiting.

June 18, 1954

I have always thought it was pointless to keep a journal. It leads to pride. I am afraid of taking myself too seriously and no longer taking seriously Christ, the Lord. And too, a daily journal inclines to introspection.

Still, today I am led to write down certain worries when they occur to me. Written analysis enters better into the subjective complexities of the cares of this world: simply being lucid about oneself sometimes makes it possible to eradicate them.

The further I go, the more I am struck by my tendency to think, at the heart of the most peaceful situations, about the burdens I have to bear. I am unable to entrust them constantly to the Lord of my life. This inclination is certainly due to the discovery I made, when I was young, of a whole tragic dimension of life too burdensome for my age. I received an idealistic and moralistic education. By "moralistic" I mean a very noble puritan upbringing, but one far away from day-to-day realities.

Ill-prepared to accept in a positive way the struggle of existence and still less the discovery of my humanity, I dealt with them on my own. That is what causes this propensity to fear, in the midst of the purest joys, an event that could diminish gladness.

When I return from a trip, I expect to hear bad news. I know well that, during the last war, I could not return home without something having happened. Will the day arrive when I accept that my joy will last?

Is there anyone more loved than I am?

I am surrounded by people, most of whom are full of charity and attentiveness. There is a bouquet of flowers on my table; I did not have to pick them.

So live from joy alone, whenever it is granted. I will be stronger to stand the blows or to support the many people who come to me, exhausted and overwhelmed.

June 19, 1954

I have to go to Bourges[1] this evening. I don't like to leave Taizé during this festival of nature.

In my youth, I rooted myself in a particular place. Today I need to become as attached as I can to Taizé. I still see too easily the disadvantages of the village of Taizé, its isolation, whereas I should be giving thanks. All I ask of the Lord is to live the present day with joy.

---

1. A city in central France about 250 kilometers from Taizé.

Thirteen years ago I preached on this topic: give thanks for today; who knows what tomorrow brings? I am surprised that I have scarcely put into practice those words that seemed so essential.

This notebook must allow me to take stock of my life, to insist on what must last, to recall truths that I consented to and then neglected.

The regularity of a journal would have helped me to return to this or that value, to build up little by little the unity of the personality in Christ.[2]

In the combat to be waged at the heart of the Church, I am worried and troubled. A letter, a conversation, make me fear the struggle.

This morning, read in *Christianisme au xxᵉ siècle* an article about Taizé. The bishop of Autun is put in an awkward situation. I already envisage the worst, that our relationship will become strained.[3]

Meditating on the first chapter of the letter to the Philippians is relevant to my fear of conflict. For the battle, make use of the best weapon of all—the peace of Christ.

"Stand firm, contending with one spirit and one mind for the faith of the Gospel, not intimidated in any way by your opponents." If I took these words out of context, I could provide schismatics with good arguments. No, these words have meaning only if we remember that the fullness of joy consists in being of "one mind . . . having the same purpose, leaving no place for party spirit."

2. This attempt to find the basic lines of force of his life so as to return to them constantly was a concern of Brother Roger's from an early age. It found its clearest expression in the *Rule of Taizé*.

3. *Christianisme au xxᵉ siècle* was a Protestant weekly that published, on June 17, 1954, an article by Raoul Stephan. It presented the choices of Taizé regarding celibacy and liturgical life in a positive light, but stated that the bishop of Autun, the Catholic diocese in which Taizé was located, should not see this as "a first step towards the Roman church."

June 1954

If there is a mixture of joy and fear in me, in the final analysis I lean towards joy. The more I advance, the more peace and joy are intimately linked. The one does not exist without the other. There is a need for peace so that my joy can last.

Agitated joys, tumultuous joys, I am afraid of you. I am mistrustful; behind your disguise, disorder lies hidden.

There are situations, communion in the sufferings of our neighbor, which are able to take away joy, but not peace.

The source of all joy remains inexhaustible. O Jesus, my joy![4]

This morning, happiness of heaven and of earth. Nothing more to be desired. I wanted to hold on to each minute.

But the evil genie of our financial difficulties assails me. This time I managed to escape without wasting any time.

There is a time for everything, a time for calculating and thinking about the state of our funds, a time for joy and another for toil.

During the past year I have often said to myself: I am filled to overflowing. In my youth I responded to the call of a common life, after first being afraid of it, it is true. Then I thought I would only be able to prepare the way; others would enter. Now I am 39 years old and prior of a community of twenty-five brothers. The breach has been made; now it is up to us to continue.

June 23, 1954

The festive joy continues. Never has our countryside seemed to me more adorned, more hospitable, more fresh and radiant. The May showers have played their part. I grumbled enough then to be able to rejoice today.

Yesterday evening, I was so fascinated by the soft hues of the sunset that I was surprised to find myself saying: this paradise is enough for me.

4. Brother Roger is quoting here the well-known hymn, *Jesu meine Freude*, turned into a chorale by Johann Sebastian Bach.

Repeated discovery of this pagan soul in my spontaneous reactions.

I think back to my visit to Pastor X the other day. Entering his home, I was humiliated by the miserable living conditions in which he is required to live. It may be admissible for the pastor, but his children did not receive a vocation to poverty by their birth. Silent revolts against God are being prepared.

The pastor and his wife bear within them a suffering, not to say a defeat. They explain that they have to hold out at all costs in a vast Catholic region where there are only one hundred Protestant families. The Catholicism there is, supposedly, superstitious.

I ask them: is there a biblical, a liturgical renewal among the Catholics? Yes, but only among an elite.

So why not support that elite? It undoubtedly enjoys the trust of the so-called superstitious Catholic majority, more than a handful of Protestants completely cut off from it.

The pastor and his wife are both people of unquestionable value.

Do we have the right to require from them such tension for a cause that today may no longer be justified: to keep alive, alongside the so-called "Roman" Christians, a tiny flock to which the Gospel is preached with no support from the mass of Christians? Is it permissible to waste one's energy when, at the heart of the Roman church itself, there are at present Christians who militate for the Gospel to be proclaimed in its purity? One day courageous men will have to solve this tragic dilemma.

The pastor gives me a tour of his town. He wanted to show me some vestiges of the Reformation. I suffered to see such an intelligent man willing to focus his interest on such a brief period of Church history, as though since the Reformation nothing essential had taken place.

And I guessed what the consequences of such an attitude would be. Could it be that Christian minorities can survive only by abandoning the universality of the Church?

June 25, 1954

On the way to Paris. The meeting I have to preside preoccupies me. I hate all its "psychic"[5] content. How far I am from the ministry that is incumbent on me.

June 30, 1954

A particularly difficult stay in Paris!

On my return, a letter informs me that the couple X have separated. I love them both so much that their distress has a deep impact on me. I cannot fault the wife for having left her husband, a man too complicated for her simple nature. She must have had a nervous breakdown. But can I be happy that she finds consolation in a friend whom she will marry? Why did she not have confession in order to free herself fifteen years ago? She did not speak about her husband to anyone, in order not to ruin the trust that his friends had in him.

Yes, knowing how simple and honest she is, I am relieved to see that she is not alone in her turmoil. But then I am in contradiction with the Gospel. The unity of a couple is indissoluble. And in spite of the Gospel I cannot banish the thought that her heart is large enough to love both her friend and her former husband. She undoubtedly thinks of him as a child mortally contagious for her. I am sure that, were it socially acceptable, she would see him again, once she has recovered, but as her sick child and no longer as her spouse.

He is crushed. I wrote to him, trying to convince him to go on with his work. He is more likely to recover in that way than by dwelling on his pain. I assured him that I was weeping with him: strange, since I am unable to shed tears in public.

I thought of my brother Max the whole day as well. I know he is downcast and I must continually pick myself up in order not to

---

5. Brother Roger uses this word with its New Testament meaning, found notably in Saint Paul and Saint James. It refers to what is this-worldly and human as opposed to what is spiritual, from God. See 1 Cor 15:42–49; Jas 3:15.

be disheartened out of sympathy for him. That would help neither of us.

July 1, 1954

Max phones me. Today he was reflecting on my inner journey. He thinks that the trial has changed me to such an extent that it is hard for him to recognize in me the person I was. He wants to be generous in return.

Knowing that my support is helpful to him is a source of incomparable delight. In addition, these days I have sensed so strongly the friendship of all my brothers.

July 16, 1954

I have written nothing for the last two weeks. Knowing that someone has read my journal keeps me from noting down anything more in it.

July 19, 1954

Received yesterday a priest of the *Mission de France*.[6] Together with a young parish priest he serves a region of the Creuse[7] with 4500 inhabitants; his parish is 45 kilometers long from one end to the other. For six years now, he has been celebrating Mass every morning alone. On Sunday there are a few women, never any men.

He lives in total indigence. He obviously does not eat his fill every day, and yet he seems to be in good form. Before he left, I wanted him to have a hearty snack. He was unable to eat his bread and apologized for his slowness.

6. A movement in the French Catholic church, begun during World War II, to prepare priests to go to dechristianized areas of the country, in order to spread the Gospel and animate parish communities while living a simple life close to the people.

7. A mountainous region in central France, relatively poor and underpopulated.

I asked him what kept him going all alone, without the support of a living parish community. He replied: the real presence of Christ in the Eucharist.

There is no sentimentality in him. His manly expression shone through a smile that rose from the depths of his being. In his look, in his attitude, suffering for others was joined to the joy of Christ.

I remain struck by the holiness of a modern man, aware of the problems of the present day, audacious in his ministry. Collaborating with the Center for Pastoral Liturgy, he is able once a year to welcome the parishioners of the twelve villages he serves (sixty inhabitants and twenty vacationers) for the Easter vigil mass.

He does not view his own situation as similar to that of Bernanos's country priest.[8] For him the country priest was too focused on his own suffering.

July 21, 1954

A day of great tension yesterday. The ceasefire in Indochina has to be signed, otherwise the war will become international. I think of all those here for whom Indochina means separation from a loved one and for those, over there, for whom it means deadly battles.

Stayed up till midnight to listen to the special programs on the radio. There is an immense hope that today the ceasefire will be announced.[9]

8. Reference to the well-known novel of Georges Bernanos, *The Diary of a Country Priest*, published in 1936.

9. The Indochina War (1946-1954) pitted the French government against the Vietnamese nationalists under Ho Chi Minh. The agreement signed this day in Geneva divided the country into two zones, with a view to an eventual reunification. The agreement never took hold, and the conflict escalated into the Vietnam War (1955-1975), with the United States replacing the French.

July 1954

Suffering from toothaches. One is not oneself in such states. Spent the morning in bed, ailing and groggy, without being able to read.

July 1954

Hesitating over an article to be written. What good will it do? There are already so many publications. What's the use of adding one more to the mass of Christian writings?[10]

At present I would like to focus on my ministry to the brothers: conversations, correspondence. That is my primary task, of course, but it does not fill my life fully. I would like to meditate more on the Bible and also renew my education. I have the ambition to learn English once again. But I do not manage to see the necessity of this program and to take it seriously. And so I never get down to it properly.

At present I would like to make a try: these pages will be useful for me in this sense. In a previous notebook I wrote about my difficulty of finding a full ministry. That task seems to be achieved. God has answered me beyond all my hopes. I have never been strongly disciplined. I can make great efforts, but I always need to be stimulated by an event. So, in general, I only prepare a sermon at the last minute.

But for the time being I would like to submit conscientiously to an inner examination and faithfully note down my daily program, my work.

Concern for the unity of the personality. Living out our original rule of life. Inner silence. Joy, simplicity, mercy.[11]

---

10. The article appeared in 1955 in issue no. 33 of the review *Verbum Caro*, entitled "*Naissance de communautés dans les Églises de la Réforme*" ("The Birth of Communities in the Churches of the Reformation").

11. The *Rule of Taizé* takes up three maxims that were important for Brother Roger from the beginning: "Throughout your day, let the Word of God breathe life into work and rest. Maintain inner silence in all things so as to dwell in Christ. Be filled with the spirit of the beatitudes: joy, simplicity, mercy."

September 25, 1954

Many Christians claim to possess the true way of praying. Some are sure that their prayer is not authentic unless it springs spontaneously from the heart. They consider those who pray using the age-old prayers of the People of God to be formalistic. Having practiced both styles of prayer, my conclusion is that my indifference or my fervor are just as much at ease in one as in the other.

Undated

The further I go in my vocation, the more it becomes impossible for me to neglect world history and not to take its suffering seriously.

I have never read so many newspapers and magazines.

Daily news opens up distant horizons to me.

Henceforth the evolution of human life is going to change more and more rapidly. Population increase alone will cause frames of reference and institutions to break down. Become informed, look at social situations dispassionately, to help the younger generation enter into a new order. Will Christians, generally behind the times, be ready when the time comes?

May 4, 1955

My past life has been dominated by a trial. A trial of strength. A trial of suffering.

A trial of strength to remain faithful to the vocation to which the Lord of the Church has called me and about which I have no doubts. A trial of suffering to bear, at the very heart of this vocation, a cross under the weight of which I could only collapse.

Is it a mirage, or have my prayers been heard? I see vanquished before me the enemy who laid me low and terrified me down to my very depths.

I hardly dare recall that night when, pushing my bed against the door, I expected the worst. Then, just as I fell asleep, the door opened.

And then, only silence. My terror suddenly turned into bitterness against God, who permitted this torment.

Jesus. You loved me first. I give you thanks. I cry out: praised be the Lord and I am delivered from my enemies.

Praise causes the tempter to back off and the joy of gratefulness drives him away. So I bless the Father, the Son and the Holy Spirit.

By the cross of Jesus I praise the Lord.

With Jesus, I carried my cross.

With him, I will carry it.

It is not heavy.

And so my soul exults.

It sings . . .. And my enemies are scattered and flee.

1958–1959

There are no journals extant for the years from May 1955 to April 1958. Was Brother Roger unwilling to keep for posterity what he may have written at that time?

Three notebooks exist covering the years from April 29, 1958 to August 12, 1963, with significant gaps. Some pages are dated; other entries are left undated. The writing is spontaneous, unpremeditated; sometimes one page corrects another.

In these years Taizé began to be better known, not just in the French and Swiss Protestant world, but in many places and churches. The drama of divided Christians, the Algerian War, questions about the community's lifestyle and, inevitably, personal meditations occupy the mind and the pen of the prior of Taizé. Surprisingly, the election of Pope John XXIII and the first audience Brother Roger had with him immediately afterwards, which was to prove so important for the history of Taizé, find no echo in these pages.

April 29, 1958

On my table a letter from Rome, asking the question: when are you coming? I believe in the value of dialogue with men involved in the workings of the Roman curia. But I am restrained by the fact that each time we travel to Italy some of our Protestant friends are upset.[1] I will put it off once again. But I do so with difficulty, because such renunciation only maintains us in our mutual intransigence.

One thought keeps coming back: after four centuries of division among Christians, without a sudden influx of grace, it will take generations to prepare the roads leading to visible unity.

In the eighteen years since I set out on this road, I have seen people enthusiastic about the cause. In the postwar period, there were reawakenings of the Christian consciousness. Those who had suffered together in the camps were sometimes unable to tolerate denominational differences any longer. Today those same men are lukewarm. There is disappointment caused by what has not been possible.

Today, more than ever I believe in the necessity of small groups of Christians on fire with an ecumenical flame; in such groups, the main thing is to ensure a continuity.

During the years when our foundation was beginning, I smiled when people said to me, "You have to build for centuries to come." I was too opposed to institutions to take seriously the continuity of our community after the first generation.

Today I say to myself: only several generations of men and women, attached with all the fibers of their being to the search for unity, will be able to pass through the ups and downs of the ecumenical vocation. For these men and women, our young communities must be focal points that pass on the flame.

---

1. Brother Roger's first visit to Rome, together with Brother Max, was in 1949; the brothers had an audience with Pope Pius XII.

April 30, 1958

In my Christian life, I am aware that I fumble around. There is a key element that I would like to interiorize more each day: mercy, the spirit of forgiveness.

For the rest, I notice progress and setbacks, emphasis first on one aspect then on another. Recently a concern for authenticity has filled my heart. I cannot speak about Christian unity or pray for it if I do not tend towards an effective unity among brothers in our life together.

May 1, 1958

Having Alain[2] alongside me, caring and tranquil, is of incomparable value to me. I withstand many trials when I know he is there.

May 2, 1958

Finished reading *Madeleine et André Gide*, by Jean Schlumberger.[3]

I appreciated the author, his surprising attentiveness to these individuals whom he understood better than they understood themselves. The rehabilitation of an ineffable love.

But, despite the author's striving to have us think well of them, Gide inspires rancor and bitterness in me. Basing one's happiness on another person's suffering and, still more, on the suffering of

2. Alain Giscard (1929–), a Frenchman who entered the community in 1949 after witnessing the life-commitment of the first seven brothers at Easter of that year, one of whom was his older brother Robert.

3. André Gide (1869–1951) was one of the most important French writers of the early twentieth century, the recipient of the Nobel Prize for Literature in 1947. What interested Brother Roger in him, aside from his prodigious literary talent, was his concern for authenticity, and undoubtedly also the fact that both had suffered from a strict and moralistic Protestant upbringing. That search for authenticity, however, led Gide to advocate and practice pederasty, whereas it led Brother Roger in a totally different direction. Schlumberger's book explains that Gide's marriage to his cousin Madeleine Rondeau was not consummated, although they were never formally divorced.

someone who is weak and who would no longer have anyone to rely on, evokes in me revolt and disgust.

Some speak of a successful divorce. Do they measure the quantity of suffering lying beneath that happiness? Human happiness built on a wounded sensibility has nothing to do with joy.

May 3, 1958

Took a walk on Mont Saint-Romain with Robert.[4] Ten years ago, we came up here together; his decision was imminent. We read the prologue to the Rule of Saint Benedict. We read it again today.

Beforehand, even though nothing had prepared us for this, we both agreed to keep an inner silence for the next ten years. Our unity must grow in peace. Enough of those hortatory speeches where each of us uses pedagogical methods to try and change the other.

Received a letter from Pierre Bourguet[5] this morning. I no longer expected from him a little trap set for me. I hope I can give him a good reply, concerned only for the unity of the Church. In this case I do not think I am being cowardly by making a one-sided concession.

May 4, 1958

Soon it will be Pentecost, when the Holy Spirit, Christ living in his church, is invoked upon the church. Grant me, Lord, your life in me so that I may not be a being of outer appearances.

---

4. Robert Giscard (1922–1993), the fifth brother to enter the community and the first Frenchman. Mont Saint-Romain is the tallest peak in the vicinity of Taizé (579 meters above sea level).

5. President of the National Council of the Reformed Church of France.

May 6, 1958

Guy Boerwinckel, a friend of ours, arrived last night from Holland. Conversations with him this morning on the terrace. We have the same concerns.

I explained to him the two underlying tendencies among us: some want to take "the narrow road," with no discernment beforehand; others place the emphasis on the importance of being present in the world before any other choices are made.

In the first group, there is an authentic desire to respond to the Gospel's call to choose the "narrow paths that lead to life."[6] But is there not also, in this aspiration, something other than a concern for authenticity according to the Gospel? Does not a character trait also play a role here, one that is a burden on other temperaments that are more nuanced, more able to practice a certain detachment concerning choices? I sometimes wonder whether they are not fooling themselves when they think they have taken the narrow path. If it corresponds to a natural tendency in them, what is supernatural about their behavior?

The first group cherishes the prayer robe, the garment that marks us visibly in our vocation. The second group fears the separation from other people that such a clear sign would bring about. The first would like the length or the number of prayer services to increase; the second, without looking for a minimum, fear an overload.

I can well believe that the conflict here is between two different temperaments. But I can't help noticing that, in times of crisis, the first ones can easily impress the whole group. If, at these times, they exert pressure, they eliminate a necessary tension from the community.

At that moment, the equilibrium is destroyed. There will be fewer apparent shocks—although that remains to be seen—but a flame will have been extinguished.

---

6. Matt 7:14.

This is how, it seems to me, in the great cenobitic[7] tradition, anxious members were able to create a bad conscience in more placid people and gradually impose on them frameworks, a host of rules. As a result of the tenacious will of legalistic minds, custumals[8] were overloaded in the course of the ages.

May 7, 1958

Ever since I entered the Christian life, I have refused to attribute a literal meaning to the call to "enter through the narrow gate."[9] A road that seems to be wide may in fact be the narrow path of which the Gospel speaks. And Christ does not necessarily call us to follow a tendency that goes against our disposition.

I always remain attentive to that broad vision when a choice has to be made. I then have to protect myself, in the life of the church, from those who have a more limited outlook. Some people try to give me a bad conscience regarding my attitude of freedom towards people and things. Sometimes they have succeeded, and they still succeed, even in the name of the Gospel of Christ. But once the yoke has been cast off, I discover joyfulness at the end of the road.

Neither my vocation, at first sight so restrictive, nor the Christian life limit my joy. On the contrary. Any time the joyful freedom drawn from the very wellsprings of life in Christ is called into question, my road can only be spoilt.

May 9, 1958

Lenten pastoral letter of Cardinal Wyszyński[10]: "A persecuted church is not less holy because of this. A church devoid of all

7. Cenobitic: concerning life in community, from the Greek *koinos bios*. Brother Roger preferred it to the term "monastic."

8. Custumal: a written collection of the customs of a monastery or a manor in the Middle Ages.

9. Matt 7:13.

10. Stefan Cardinal Wyszyński (1901–1981) was the archbishop of

earthly property is still in possession of much more precious things, in other words the sacraments and prayer. Even an abandoned church—like Christ on Calvary—is still the love, the salvation and the peace of humanity."

May 10, 1958

I cannot remember ever having experienced a more radiant beginning of May. The perfumed air wafts through the house. A desert wind reaches all the way to us. Springtime may never have arrived so late. And so the happiness which causes my whole being to vibrate at every renewal is given full rein.

This very moment Daniel[11] brings me a ceramic lamp that is already mounted. [. . .]

Joyfulness sings within me. My ever deeper attachment to nature, and in particular to each tree, to each plant that adorns the garden, fills me with joy.

Trials are present each day, sometimes excruciating ones, nothing can remove them from the road, and the patience to accept them is sometimes lacking. So I know that the Lord grants to each person compensations according to his needs.

For me, strength and joy are renewed by contemplating the fruit, the flowers, the branch of a tree, a bush.

Every year I wait for the peonies to blossom. Since I was a small child, in the springtime my impatience would grow: will the peonies blossom in time for my birthday, May 12? As a child I sometimes even forced them to bloom by removing the protective petals from the flower.

Warsaw-Gniezno and the primate of Poland from 1948 until his death. A strong resister to the Communist regime, he incarnated the soul of the Polish people during those difficult years. Brother Roger attended a Mass he celebrated in Rome in 1957, saw him there during the Second Vatican Council, and met him later on a visit to Poland in 1973.

11. Daniel de Montmollin (1921–), was one of the first four brothers whom Brother Roger met in Switzerland during the war. Originally a theology student and an ordained pastor, later on he began the pottery workshop in the community and achieved international renown as a potter.

Today, I am waiting calmly and with deep joy.

Life teaches me lessons. I think that since my teenage years I have learned acceptance.

This education was possible on account of a suffering that has been constantly sharpened.

I regret nothing.

I give thanks.

May 13, 1958

Yesterday was my birthday. I wrote nothing in this notebook. I look forward to May 12 as a day full of joy. That did not happen. Painful explanations, the weight of susceptibilities. The further I go forward in life, the more I consent to passing through the small daily trials with inner peace.

May 14, 1958

The French political news is bad.[12] Keep inner peace so as not to be too affected. I keep on trusting and cannot endorse pessimistic views.

May 20, 1958

Six days without being able to note any impressions. The political tension was grave. Then there were three days in Switzerland, at the World Council of Churches, to lay out the project of a small group of brothers in Geneva. Saddened by the conversation with Pastor Visser 't Hooft.[13] He only began to understand when he realized our desire to be open to the position of the churches of the

12. On May 13, during the Algerian War for Independence, a coup d'état involving the French army took place in Algeria, creating the possibility of an insurrection in France.

13. W. A. Visser 't Hooft (1900–1985), Dutch theologian, first secretary general of the World Council of Churches in Geneva.

Reformation as well as that of the church of Rome. Like others, he is convinced that our Roman sympathies blind us.

Every trip disturbs my ability to work. I should take this into account and group my journeys together as much as I can.

May 22, 1958

Replied to Pierre Bourguet's letter. I said yes to everything. Not out of weariness, not at all, but because of the importance of unity. Unity among Christians is paramount; it is even more important than following the guidelines we set beforehand.

May 23, 1958

The joy of community prayer. I note it because it is not frequent. Looking forward to this evening's service, the peacefulness of the prayer, some of the hymns, the life of Christ among us in the church.

May 28, 1958

The agitation caused by the political events is upsetting. We fear civil war, bloodshed. I can't help noticing that I am unable to write in this notebook when the outward tensions are overpowering. I long for the situation to improve. And the fact of writing is precisely what enables me to pull myself together.

This evening at 10 p.m., the house is calm. I listen to a concerto by Handel after spending an hour outside on the terrace. On the rise facing east, I stood above the landscape, the woods in the direction of Chazelle.[14] It does good to pray there, just as it does to look at the cows, listen to their bells, examine this or that tree.

Loving God in creation calms a passion for events and beings that is too strong. Discovering the ardor that animates every

14. A village across the Grosne River, about 3 kilometers from Taizé.

season of the year, every day of the season, brings unparalleled refreshment and joy.

One season is alien to me, the months between Epiphany and the end of March. True, the trees and plants have already been bare by then for two long months, but in compensation there was the intimacy of the first cold weeks indoors, Advent, the preparations for Christmas, the joyful expectation.

I shall try to enter into the poetry of January and February. Understanding poetry, in other words creation at work, brings with it the desire to live.

Loving God in his creation, the poetry of nature.

May 30, 1958

I would like to tell Catholics, without causing them any hurt for all that: by living your faith in today's world, at the heart of society, you will bridge the gulfs much more than by trying to prove the soundness or the legitimacy of your positions.

The younger generation of non-Roman Christians looks to you, and sometimes expects you to accomplish great things for the world; in this way you will fulfill your truly catholic vocation.

This younger generation aspires to a unity of all human beings; in this respect it is sometimes demanding. It will enter into a relationship with you to the extent that it senses in you a passion for your vocation of universality, of catholicity.

Be authentic, in accord with the profession of your faith and of charity, and you will solve, more than you realize, the irresolvable drama of our divisions among Christians.

May 31, 1958

At this moment the national synod of the Reformed Church of France is meeting at Poitiers and listening to a report on Taizé. Without wishing to give this fact an importance out of proportion to reality, I think the declaration read is important. A step has been taken towards a visible unity of Christians who cannot be divided.

Some Reformed Christians barely consider us to be one of them. Are we so far from the fundamentalists of the Reformed faith? I cannot say, but what I cannot stand would be to judge one another. Our background is the same; we cannot deny it. That is already a program and one which is quite appealing.

June 2, 1958

Inner questioning: are we not accumulating the means of material security? Have we not gone beyond the limit? We ought to limit ourselves to what facilitates our work, because we do almost everything ourselves, from the purchase of provisions to the cooking of food.

I continued this inner conversation with a brother. He was reassuring. The previous day he said himself that adapting our old buildings was not very practical and that to be wealthy would mean building a spacious edifice that would correspond to our life. That's true. We have been content to make our old stones fit for habitation.

Poverty consists in setting everything in the simple beauty of creation.[15] But it means above all living in God's today. I resolve my inner conflict concerning simplicity of life by returning to some texts from our Rule. Living in the present day.

June 4, 1958

Forgiveness: if I did not forgive on account of Christ and the Gospel, I would do so in order to liberate myself. So as not to keep alive the bitterness that poisons and keeps us from loving the flower, the leaf, the dew. . . . Forgiveness, a key fact of existence.

15. See *The Rule of Taizé*, 83.

June 5, 1958

Guests find their way right up to my window, one after another. I am bothered by these repeated intrusions. I lean out to ask these unknown persons to go to the reception. But I come face to face with a humble family, who seem intimidated. I go down at once to welcome them. I want to atone for the curt tone of my first words.

I wasn't wrong: we have some of Christ's poor at our door. The mother is from Martinique, the children of mixed race. I am appalled at my earlier coldness. When will I learn to accept those who have been sent by God? Because many pass through with an unbecoming curiosity, I close up.

I wanted to make up for my first attitude by bringing some juice and biscuits. Then how moved I am a second time to learn that this family, living alone in the countryside, shares our prayer through the recording *Soli Deo gloria!*[16]

June 6, 1958

Too many Christians wear themselves out in a desperate need to legitimate the value of their own denomination. Perhaps our old Christian societies will get out of the rut in which they are sinking when the younger generations refuse to join these exhausting battles of self-justification: this young church, running towards the Lord, will draw in its wake the old world of divided Christians.

Our Protestant spirituality is focused on speech, on words, which explains its constant appeal to the mind. It has become worn out in self-defense.

Only a return to the wellsprings of the universal church (those of the East as much as those of the West) will enable us to stop giving speeches so that the light of Christ can penetrate us, not so much by speaking as by seeing, contemplating, listening.

16. *Soli Deo Gloria*, a recording made in 1955 of the daily prayer at Taizé.

June 7, 1958

Invited to dinner the plumber, the electrician, and our good friend Paul, the livestock dealer. Work relationships have not at all damaged the friendship that unites us.

Before leaving to return to our respective jobs, we were chatting on the terrace when one of our brothers, an intellectual if ever there was one, arrived in slovenly dress. The contrast between our friends, with no extensive formal education but so dignified in their bearing, and his negligence hurt me. Afterwards, I asked him to purchase a shirt and a jacket. We do not come closer to working people by our slovenliness, either in words or in dress.

June 1958

Church institutions have often sunken low (simony, etc.). But Christians have to find ways of allowing things to stand up straight again. The church advances in the midst of deep furrows.

July 10, 1958

Always the same process. After having read some pages of my journal to a brother and having heard his criticism, I have no desire any longer to jot down the daily happenings. I have stopped writing for a month now.

I spent some time at Rasses.[17] Unhelpful conditions for withdrawing and writing. Only the kitchen was heated; there was no quiet place. I tried to immerse myself in my childhood again. Some of the Swiss landscape drew me in that direction. I recalled a childhood that was happy until about the age of fifteen. Then I had to suffer the consequences of my father's problems.[18]

17. A village in the Swiss Jura mountains.

18. Brother Roger had a difficult relationship with his father, while always respecting his views, his learning, and his upright character. Following a fall from an attic and a head injury when Roger was in his teens, Pastor Schutz's character became more rigid and fearful and his ministry more difficult.

Beginning then everything grew dark, but with shafts of light: the long meditations during walks in the canton of Fribourg[19] allowed me to gain self-mastery and clear-sightedness about myself.

The positive result of this return to the past is to remind me that, in life in Christ, I have to leave father and mother behind, abandon my family to God, which in no way means a lack of affection. But how hard it is to achieve this!

When will I accept, as every adult must, the fact that my family has to live their own life? I need to mature in this outlook. I am not at all looking for a break with them but rather for an autonomy which has been slow in coming.

July 29, 1958

At the next meeting of the brothers, in September, I will bring up the question: does it happen that at certain moments we think we are at the center of the world, at least of a certain world, whether that world is called the church or bears another name?

When the human mind reaches that state of giddiness, it must quickly discover a sense of humor. Laughing heartily in order to relax.

Our friends are the ones who play the worst trick on us by lifting us up to the heights where they would like us to be. They see us as supermen, or at least exceptional men able to have a decisive influence on the present, if not on the future.

I am interested in history, but only to understand the present. In my youth I liked it because of the discoveries; I felt I was part of a vast adventure story. That time is past. In this way, after reading Dansette's[20] history of the church in France from the revolution to the present, I am more sure and understanding in my evaluation of the Catholic Christianity of France.

---

19. Switzerland is divided into cantons. The border between the canton of Vaud, largely Protestant, and the Catholic canton of Fribourg runs just above the village of Oron, where Brother Roger's father was pastor.

20. Adrien Dansette, *Histoire religieuse de la France contemporaine*, 2 vols. (Flammarion, 1948–1951).

During my trip with Max to the United States,[21] I discovered the frantic acceleration of human evolution as one of the main facts of the twentieth century.

I knew that, from Roman times, farming had scarcely evolved; it was only at the end of the nineteenth century that a new beginning occurred. I also knew that in the last ten years the evolution of agriculture in the West has been accelerating at a stupefying rate. But this journey to visit a new nation was necessary in order to realize that, in all the domains of life, the rate of evolution will get faster and faster.

That implies a transformation of human mentalities to which, as Christians, we have to respond if we really do not want to "hide our light under the bushel basket." [22]

As the years pass, my inner life changes. I cannot stand one-sided judgments. Political enthusiasms inciting people to affirmations that brook no reply hurt me. It is not that I have been or still am exempt from passionate views. But I control, or at least I try to control, every "psychic"[23] movement.

July 30, 1958

Short walk at nightfall. Once again I followed the long terrace through the vegetable garden, then I walked to the end of the enclosure among the sound of the cowbells.

Every person who has known the exhilarating experience of travel and the means of transportation that have conquered space, every person who has been intoxicated to have, on horseback, then in a car, the power to hold distances in his own hands, returns one day, if he takes the time, to rediscover that treasure never exhausted and yet on a human scale—walking.

---

21. In late 1955, Brothers Roger and Max were invited to give a series of talks in the United States by a young American Lutheran who had spent some time in Taizé.

22. Matt 5:15.

23. See note 5 for June 25, 1954.

I do not in any way underestimate the current means of transportation. But by themselves they are not sufficient to bring people and things closer in a new way.

When I drive, I spend part of my time speeding along while avoiding accidents.[24] On foot, every blade of grass and every branch welcome me. Still, after a great while without taking long walks, I have to rediscover them, learn again the art of walking.

As the years pass, my horizon widens. Having taken this road, I could no longer go forward any other way. But aside from a few long trips, I desire nothing more than our terraces, our enclosure.

July 31, 1958

A good deal of a human being's energy is dedicated to trying to achieve emotional fulfillment. When this requires an injudicious expenditure of attention, of will, and yet leads to repeated crises, wisdom consists in transcending oneself. This step is incredibly painful, so that a person often refuses to take it, for he prefers to suffer from an unhappy love, which is already no longer really a love, than to live with no hope of love at all.

August 12, 1958

After the meals, be careful not to go toward this or that brother who attracts my sympathy. Go towards the most humble, the one who is shy or reserved.

September 4, 1958

A tension concerning our vocation. Should we place the accent on contemplative life, or instead organize our life so that everything

---

24. Brother Roger's driving style was legendary. Possibly only divine intervention can explain the fact that he never had an accident!

becomes efficient? Contemplation or efficiency? To put it another way: living like the Little Brothers of Jesus or like the Jesuits?[25]

June 5, 1959

Nine months without writing anything down. And yet I consider these notes as a means of internalizing, perhaps the only one.

We have just opened a door on to the row of trees behind the house. The thought of being able to be out in nature in a flash, just by leaving my room, enchants me.

Our house has a facade which is somewhat austere, or at least proper. But there is also the matchless charm of what lies behind—the row of trees, the spacious enclosure, a place of meditative silence.

This spring Robert, as never before, has cut the lawns and cleaned every nook and cranny.

To bring order to what nature has destroyed! By the response of the first man confronted with freedom, by his choice to break with God because of the attraction of the forbidden fruit, disorder came to abide in the world and, with disorder, illness, suffering and death. Trying to re-establish a harmony which has been destroyed enables us to manifest our refusal of sin, of disorder.

In monastic life, the Benedictines have received this vocation to order, to re-establish, to build anew. The peace of their life and their sense of discretion help us to seek the simple beauty of creation.

For his part Saint Francis, with a passion for the beauty of creatures, forsook creating order and ran towards those who could not live elsewhere than in destitution. He loved the poor, while not looking down on those who were not poor at all.

---

25. The Little Brothers of Jesus are a religious congregation that attempts to live, in the footsteps of Charles de Foucauld (see note 5, p. 4), a contemplative presence among the poor by sharing their life and work with no explicit pastoral activity.

I wish, for the balance of our vocation, that these two possibilities might remain alive among my brothers: using efficient means, an ordered life, and this other possibility, the poverty of means in order to be poor among the poor, one with them.

July 2, 1959

Pride wounded. A childhood wound, similar to so many others. The lack of success, fear of humiliation. The need to know that my works follow me, are known, visible. The fear of being in competition, or at least eclipsed by someone else, if that individual elbows me out in order to take my place. All that remains murky. But I tremble to lose the joy of belonging to God.

The ego tyrannizes me with its infantile demands. I am aware of this at every moment, but the struggle is hidden and joy is absent. These days, moreover, there is an absence of joy that upsets me. I ask myself why. I don't think that my brothers are aware of it. I entrust this heavy heart to my Christ. May he fill it with light and grant me the strength to give myself.

Worrying oneself to death in order to be appreciated by many! The Gospel teaches me the opposite. No reason, even one that I could invoke in the name of the church, of its good, can subsist if it is a matter, in the final analysis, of causing the ego to triumph, of giving it a more solid base in the midst of others.

And in addition, what an impossible task is that will to be known! Let's assume that several tens of thousands of Christians appreciate my talent, and then what? And the billions of people who will never know anything about it? And those who will come after them, a century later!

The tyranny of glory that sometimes arises in me, I want to acknowledge it to myself. Lord, grant me to live nothing else than a life hidden with you in God.

To be misunderstood, even despised, but to be loved by God and by those few men placed alongside me, who sometimes know me better than I know myself.

July 1959

In the *Mémoires intérieurs* of François Mauriac[26]: "Christ in his teaching never seems to worry about our idiosyncratic tastes. Knowing the quirks of our inclinations is indifferent to him. His requirement, and this is the same for all, is that we be pure, that we give up our cravings, whatever their object may be."

In the same book, speaking of Gerard Manley Hopkins, an English poet converted to Rome under the influence of Newman, Mauriac writes: "He does not defend himself against the object of his torment. He contemplates it, faces up to it and embraces it. That is our vocation as Christians: the opposite of running away, of evasion—a hand-to-hand combat, or rather spirit to spirit."[27]

July 17, 1959

Anxiety grows and diminishes like the ebb and flow of the sea. Parts of myself remain at an infantile stage. My own conscience is stupidly dominated by other consciences, paternal recollections. I try once again to hand over to others that scum that floats to the surface: obsessional states, dreams, latent fears . . .

Always the same refusal to accept having a body. In my childhood, I was allowed to live only through ideas, ideals: a moralistic education developed the mind. Development took place at the top of the skull; the rest of the body just had to be accepted.

Christ, true man, true God, little by little teaches me through the Gospel to accept the totality of my being. I manage to believe first of all in the transfiguration of the entire being, body, soul and spirit, by the contemplation of Christ-God. In him, nothing is lost. Faults, sin, deviations, losses of all kinds are rediscovered. Let myself be transfigured gradually by the One who draws into himself the pure and the impure, the true and the unauthentic.

26. François Mauriac (1885–1970): French Catholic novelist, Nobel Prize for Literature (1952).

27. François Mauriac, *Mémoires intérieurs* (Flammarion, 1959), 190 and 146.

1961–1962

These years between the election of Pope John XXIII and the open-ing of the Second Vatican Council represent a kind of transition be-tween a more hidden life in community and a wider impact. Despite regrets within and criticisms from without, what takes precedence are reflections on the meaning of the community's life and prayer, and the commitment to the ecumenical vocation.

April 2, 1961, Good Friday

As every year, it is hard to live this Holy Week because of the austerity of the liturgy.

April 10, 1961

On Holy Saturday, a priest was determined to come and share with me some negative reactions about Taizé that he heard from pastors in Paris. It was a lot to take. But I remembered that we were at the end of Lent and it was necessary to drink this cup.

His visit taught me nothing new, but these oppositions weigh me down and they stayed with me until the great Easter liturgy.

There are times when I find the ecumenical struggle hard to bear. These days I have asked to be purified of the leaven of bitterness. I ask to learn to forgive offenses at every moment, for the grace to be refreshed by mercy. Without the spirit of mercy, constantly renewed, I would be unable to remain on my feet.

May 5, 1961

I remain slightly beneath my level. The exuberant joy of youth has been overtaken by a constant weariness that I alone am aware of; the others do not notice it. I am unable to rejoice at the great springtime that is sweeping across the earth with signs that presage fullness.

I have always felt that joy was a result of the life of Christ in me. O Jesus, my joy. Without it everything runs the risk of becoming constricted, and false problems that poison daily life can arise.

Joy is indispensable to lead others with oneself towards Christ and to drown in it the pettiness of each day. Joy is indispensable if we are to be victorious in the struggle for the unity of Christians.

That is the freedom of Christians, in spite of the evil that hampers them: they can entrust everything to Christ in order to turn towards the joys of God's kingdom, different forms of joy that extend from the communion of saints to the contemplation of God in creation.

Christians have better things to do than to let themselves be contaminated by the bitterness of the day; they are enabled to return incessantly to the joy of the Beatitudes.

As the years pass, exuberant joy gives way to a stronger joy, implanted in peace and serenity. Above all, do not regret the absence of inadvertent bursts of a joy that is hard to contain. To each day its troubles, its weariness, but also its joy.

I sometimes wonder about the attraction of the intimate life of a household.

Read with enthusiasm a life of Tolstoy. I would happily dive into the letters of Ramuz.[1]

I need to organize the intimacy of a household for my brothers. But is there an incompatibility between our monastic vocation and this need for family life, whose constituent parts are not at all inspired by monasticism? There is this constant dilemma in me.

The result is that sometimes I remove a lot of furniture from the house and, at other times, I bring in other articles of furniture.

I have come to the conclusion that there are times in the year, the season of Advent or of Epiphany, where it is good and necessary to decorate the house, to remove all the signs of Puritanism or Jansenism,[2] and other times when it is important to be more austere. On the other hand, it is good that some areas, full of intimacy and even of memories, always remain.

1. Charles Ferdinand Ramuz (1878–1947), Swiss novelist and poet.

2. Jansenism: A theological movement influential in France from the seventeenth century onwards, which radicalized the positions of Saint Augustine to emphasize human sinfulness and the weakness of the will. It was promoted notably by a group of Catholics who gravitated around the convent of Port-Royal-des-Champs. As a child, Brother Roger listened with great interest to family readings of Saint-Beuve's history of Port Royal. Much of his spiritual life can be seen as an attempt to free himself from an overly pessimistic and guilt-ridden piety by emphasizing God's forgiveness and joy as a hallmark of the Christian life.

Unlimited gratefulness for the deep friendship that unites Max and me. A pure and serene friendship if ever there was one. An incomparable grace in a life where all one fears is the separation that comes with death.

This year, signs of some good results of our ecumenical vocation abound. And yet the element of success that they represent gives rise to some agitation, to jealousy. I understand the annoyance felt by certain workers for unity who are living their vocation faithfully and do not enjoy the same human renown as Taizé.

At the same time, perhaps because of the fact that some people are upset, and also because I do not want to place my trust in visible successes, I am well aware of the enormous work for unity that still lies before us. This work grows with the years and our limits become still more obvious.

The fact that we have achieved certain results does not at all lead to a sense of having reached the goal. It is as if everything still needed to be done. As a result, more than ever I cling to God's hope to unite his scattered flock.

We cannot do much for this unity. That plunges me into darkness and forces me to rely on faith alone: "I call and he answers me."[3] Calling to God in the prayer of the divine office, the Psalms in particular, that is what is sure. But on account of the human pessimism which, at a time like this, could gain the upper hand, we also sing the final victory in hymns and spiritual songs.

In this respect, the hymns from the Reformation have never seemed to me such a valuable complement to praying the Psalms. They are the most precious treasure bequeathed by the Reformation to fortify our devotion.

May 6, 1961

For a long time I have been convinced that to each age there corresponds an activity, a fulfillment. Even the age of retirement, the

---

3. See Pss 4:1; 55:16; 119:145.

advanced age of someone in their eighties, must have a goal, limited by the person's abilities. Ending life simply by waiting to die and enter the eternal life that follows places people in an inhuman condition. A specific goal always remains necessary.

No time for idleness, but only to relax and be restored, or as athletes would say, to recuperate.

The unity of the personality requires being steadfast in one's earliest commitments, taking responsibility on every occasion for the decisions of the past. So, since at the age of twenty-five I decided to settle in the village of Taizé, I cannot call this decision of my youth into question in any way, even by a regret.

I don't know why I still have this nagging regret that I didn't go to live close to Macon,[4] a region more welcoming, more cheerful and more alive than our valley of the Grosne. God alone can free me from this remorse that has returned almost every day for the last year or two.

"O God, come to my assistance; O Lord make haste to help me."[5] Dispose my heart to love this area and to give thanks in the depths of my being.

May 8, 1961

The futility of regretting. In regret the inner self disintegrates. There is a sterility in the mind of the one who, far from being invigorated, gets bogged down in reflections where he reconstructs a situation that is over and done with without getting any good out of it.

There are childhoods that invite unconscious remorse; we always wish to begin again in order to do better. But what do we ever achieve really well? In the realm of morality everything we do is more-or-less.

Regret makes sterile. Regret debilitates.

---

4. A town 35 kilometers southeast of Taizé.

5. Ps 70:1.

Do not confuse regret and repentance. It's true that the two are linked. There is regret in repentance, but repentance cannot turn into regret. I see repentance as a powerful act, a turning back on oneself which is not protracted, but which leads to two steps: reparation whenever possible (in the old Christian language this is called "penance"), and handing over to God the evil we have done in order to be completely unburdened, absolved, forgiven.

In *Foma Gordeyev*, Gorky[6] tells of the destruction of Ignatius's boat by ice on the Volga. Ignatius, a miser and jealous of every ruble, accepts this loss at once. He knows that regret would be useless, and he is already convinced and reassures himself that by working he will be able to rebuild.

There are beings with whom we are deeply involved and who constantly destroy. It is useless to complain about the harm they cause; all we can do is limit the damage.

Weep, O child of the earth, people are abandoning God. The silence spreads more and more. And the little sparks of light are going out.

Having gone through some very bad years, "struck down by God and humiliated,"[7] at present I am gradually finding peace. The years of founding the community remain, in some respects, an almost unbearable struggle.

Those who consider themselves free spirits in the sexual realm should be wary of their lack of inner freedom in this regard. Through a certain freedom of expression, by making use of a kind of vulgarity, a person can camouflage a great inner disorder in the life of the senses.

6. An early novel by Maxim Gorky (1868–1936), a Russian writer and political activist. He lived much of his life in exile, but returned to the Soviet Union before his death.

7. Isa 53:4.

Personal prayer supports two initiatives: on the one hand communion with God, by activating our fervor, and on the other communion with other people, by enabling us to shine with God's light, to be men of God and thus men of peace.

By it we enter into the consenting that is necessary every day—consenting to our religious state, to our aging, to missed opportunities.

Personal prayer, in the form of short invocations or a sign of the cross when we are alone or at work, leads to inner silence.

Return to the spirit and the letter of our Rule: maintain inner silence in all things, assisted by the prayer of the Name of Jesus, by psalms read or learnt by heart or perhaps sung.

May 10, 1961

Received a phone call inviting me to a Franco-German conference of journalists. I am asked to describe the situation of Christians today regarding ecumenism. Every time I am parachuted into an intellectually superior milieu I flounder. I will see what brother is up to this kind of contact.

April 1962

The detachment that is growing in me regarding the surrounding countryside impresses me. We are in the middle of April without a true springtime. I find it harder than in the past to stand these long winters out in the country and I feel even more strongly how alien I am in this land on which, one day, I decided to live for ever.

Giving up our farm to a cooperative was costly for me, but there too the immoderate love of having some farmland of my own, everything I wished for as a youth, is somewhat disappointed. The monastic vocation is perhaps given new value by this progressive detachment. [8]

8. In 1962, five farmers in the area along with the community formed a cooperative farm, the COPEX; each participant contributed their material

In addition, concerning our property, I was the first one who wanted it to go to the local collectivity, a solution for the future.

I am well aware that if the farm had been a small ordered world, with a limited number of cows, heifers and one or two horses, I would have found in it a support, a rootedness that I always thought was necessary and of which I would not have been ashamed.

What is oppressive in our valley is the dark line of mountains to the east. That chain cuts me of from the plains of the Saone River, the major lines of communication. Moreover, the north-south orientation of the valley leaves it open to the winds, the cold that keeps nature from bursting forth and speeds its death in the autumn. And finally, that chain of mountains hides the Jura Mountains and the Alps.

April 1962

Is my Tolstoyan ideal of life in the country compatible with monastic life? I never saw them as mutually exclusive and, in fact, there is a balance between them that has sustained our existence from the beginning.

I am not a romantic about the monastic vocation. For me it is becoming more and more the offering of my life for the visible unity of Christians. Present in the church on several occasions during the day, I know that God has his eyes upon us.

All that remains is to say to him: look, Lord, upon your people. Look on our little community that is imploring unity; look on us, for we are poor in material and spiritual resources; look also on divided Christians, whose possibilities are so poor precisely because of their divisions.

---

and livestock. In addition, the community gave the COPEX fourteen hectares which belonged to it.

April 15, 1962, Palm Sunday

Rain mixed with snow, a dark sky, all these things together call us to live within, indoors and within ourselves.

How pleasant is the relationship with my brothers! Time passes and the bonds between us are more solid, the trust more authentic.

May 1962

Radiant light of May. Once again I can write sitting under the lime tree at the end of the row.

But suddenly I catch myself dreaming of other skies, always the same ones, beyond the hill to the east. It is as if I were uprooted from the civilized land of my childhood, also to the east, and aspired to fresh springs, to abundant water, to cheerful and well-ordered surroundings. All that is the "old self." I only escape this vague nostalgia by entering fully into the vocation of a brother and prior of Taizé.

The chastity of celibacy is related to a catholic and ecumenical vocation. A man who lives in chastity is a man who opens his arms and does not close them on anyone. Chastity excludes making another person a captive of oneself.

Open to all, to every concern, able to exercise a welcome, as far as his or her own limitations permit, the man or woman who lives in chastity becomes a truly catholic person.

Consenting to the yes and the love of a faithful heart and letting this consent penetrate the deepest reaches of oneself is a process that gradually commits the totality of one's being. And then chastity, and the struggle it involves, is transformed into an unsuspected dynamism.

A person who has consented to chastity, even outside of the response to a mysterious call from Christ, is endowed with a particular strength.

Those who are committed to chastity are unsettled by the secularization of today's world. Every day the press, television, books, have a strong impact on their lives.

1962

Consent to a flight into the wilderness, at Taizé, when confronted with a world that calls. "Lord, it is to you that I have fled."[9]

1962

Whenever I appeal to a tangible resonance of God within me, my soul becomes worried that I do not belong to God.

A great deference towards sacred signs, a great devotion emphasized by gestures, without seeking anything in return.

"My soul rests in peace in God alone."[10] Base one's life on the reality that everything is fulfilled in him, even when nothing makes his action visible. Seek peace, serenity after the long battle.

1962

"Put yourself under your own feet": in this way John XXIII concluded a conversation with a Catholic ecumenist. Wishing to indicate a concrete step to those involved in the quest for unity among Christians, the pope, in a gesture of humiliation where he was the first to commit himself, insisted: put yourself under your own feet.

We church leaders are hypersensitive about what concerns our own denominations. We tell ourselves: our ancestors defended certain positions; they were outstanding; they sometimes suffered a great deal. Heirs to a deposit of faith, are we going to let our spiritual patrimony be dilapidated?

Looking back to a past of combats and tears paralyzes our energies. When our energies become overwrought our sensibility

9. Ps 143:9.
10. Psalm 62:1.

quickly overflows; to avoid the suffering of a wounded sensibility it turns inward and withdraws into itself, and without realizing it we become oversensitive.

Hence the very apt advice: put yourself under your own feet. Refuse to take into account the wounds that come from the incomprehension of other Christians and, even more important, refuse to make the quest for unity your own personal cause: it is not my own self that counts, but the totality of Christians who make up the Body of Christ.

Since the Renaissance all we have been doing is justifying our sectarian assertiveness, whether denominational or political.

1963

January 1, 1963

Christian freedom. The only one who can free us is Christ Jesus. Through him, the Living One, we can remain free in the face of disappointments and contradictions. We are masters of everything when, in certain circumstances, our choice leads us to accept a certain death to ourselves, to a part of ourselves.

We should not confuse giving "free rein" to our temperament with this freedom of choice in the name of Christ.

In the name of Christ we do not want to subjugate anyone, to make anyone a captive of ourselves. Giving free rein to our temperament, to our anger, bitterness, and fleshly imagination means subjugating others and ourselves and making our neighbor a captive of ourselves.

When I discipline my body and make it my slave,[1] subjecting it to myself by fasts and vigils, this is only out of love for Christ Jesus. No one else is able to lead me to this sacrifice, to this death to myself.

A master of everything, I submit to everyone out of love. Christian liberty is the expression of an antinomy. Free with respect to everything and to all, I submit to everyone. The apostle says it better than anyone: "Though I am free with respect to all, I have made myself a slave to all."[2] "Owe no one anything, except to love one another."[3]

March 26, 1963

I am passionately interested in all that is human; my whole being is awakened by it.

---

1. 1 Cor 9:27.
2. 1 Cor 9:19.
3. Rom 13:8.

March 1963

Since the Council began,[4] I think that one of the great questions that the church of tomorrow will have to deal with will be that of the church of the poor.

In the Middle Ages, the Gospel created a great sensitivity to the communication of material goods. The standard of living of different people in a city was fairly identical.

It was the rediscovery of Roman law that slowly transformed church law, with the result that "mine" and "yours," the right to property, would little by little be justified. But there is no fellowship as brothers and sisters except where sharing is visibly expressed.

June 1963

I am so attached to Taizé with all the fibers of my being that being cut off brutally, without being able to communicate easily, as is the case now in Forclaz[5] for a time of rest, tears in me that flesh and that being which forms one with the community, the different places, the church, and especially the community prayer.

I love to have with me the remarkable brothers who are around me here, to live with them in the rhythm of community life. But I wonder whether vacations are a worthwhile option for monks, or at least for their prior.

The death of Pope John XXIII touches me in the very depths of my being. A human security has suddenly been removed and I realize now what a support he was for our vocation—and what a father, too.

4. Brother Roger, together with Brother Max, was invited as an observer to the Second Vatican Council as a special guest of the Roman Secretariat for Christian Unity. For four years he assisted at every session of the council in St. Peter's Basilica, and the community welcomed many bishops and experts to their table for meals in their Roman apartment.

5. A village in the Swiss canton of Valais.

June 1963

Pride and humility. Go more and more deeply into the meaning of these terms. I know that pride and vanity are poison for Church leaders. How can I speak to them if I and my brothers fall into the same trap?

There is a gratification of pride that momentarily offers a peace of mind, but the need reappears and is even more pressing. The urge for power even led to the building of basilicas "in the name of the Lord."

I have still not come to terms with the construction of our Church of Reconciliation, whose dimensions are out of proportion to our intentions. Can I ask the builder to create inside it places of worship for others, to reduce the interior dimensions?[6]

June 1963

The Mother of Christ, the Virgin Mary can only be venerated in a deep relationship with her Son and set in the communion of all the holy witnesses to Christ.

Catholicism has often been tempted to take the Virgin out of that close communion with the whole church, to isolate her and to present her all alone, pulling her out of her situation of humility.

Protestantism, in its turn, by isolating Christ and by presenting him with no relationship to the whole church, has taken away

6. In the early years, community prayers were held in the small twelfth-century Romanesque church in the village of Taizé. By the 1960s, it had become inadequate for the number of worshipers at certain times of the year. A new church was designed by Brother Denis, an architect by training, and constructed with the help of German volunteers from *Aktion Sühnezeichen*, an organization founded to sponsor signs of reparation in places touched by the war. The Church of Reconciliation was formally inaugurated on August 6, 1962 in the presence of numerous church leaders. Although he had been kept fully informed of the ongoing project, Brother Roger was shocked by the final dimensions of the building, having imagined a more modest edifice. Ironically, ten years later the new church proved to be too small and had to be extended at first by circus tents, then by more permanent constructions, in order to contain the vast numbers of young people coming to Taizé.

the means of reaching him through the communion of saints, of the church.

July 9, 1963

Received among others the Spanish priest Alfonso Roig. I tried to explain to him my worry in the face of that need for power that constantly arises in each person, without our being aware of it. Living the spirit of the Beatitudes[7] is all we can do.

Sometimes, too often, there is a piercing pain in my heart. I don't know how to get rid of it; prayer is not enough to remove it. Why this sempiternal regret at having chosen the site of Taizé? It is not the fact of having suffered here because suffering, on the contrary, creates an attachment to the places where it was experienced.

There are topics that benefit by being cast far away from oneself: the temptations of regret in particular.

Just as there is an exercise, a discipline, that consists in chasing away all fleshly desires and imagination, it is required of me as well to cast far from me all the regrets that imprison me in a childish attitude.

July 11, 1963

Max has arrived at Montreal.[8] I have been praying constantly for that beloved brother, because flying is so hard for him.

I have to struggle within myself to find more solitude. Too many requests for meetings. To find myself once again.

---

7. Matt 5:1–12, the beginning of the Sermon on the Mount, was from the beginning a key text for the community. See *The Rule of Taizé*, 53.

8. He had gone to the fourth world conference of "Faith and Order," the doctrinal commission of the World Council of Churches; Catholic observers took part for the first time as well.

Tears sometimes come upon me suddenly, again today in church. And also the day before yesterday, kneeling before the icons in my room. It was the gentle love of Christ that penetrated me down to my feelings. Why so seldom? But shortly afterwards, I lost my temper because of an annoyance, and I should have asked for forgiveness, I think.

Don Alfonso Roig is afraid lest the spirit of the Beatitudes, which he discovered on our hill, be spoilt by the new Church of Reconciliation.

The visibility of institutions through buildings is a daunting sign. Denis, our architect brother,[9] to whom I confided the wound constantly reopened in me by the building of the church, manifested the spirit of the Beatitudes so authentically. Just looking at his face confirmed me in the certainty that he was not mistakenly leading us along a road where the institution would be sufficient unto itself.

July 12, 1963

The ideal of the Poverello was so extreme that it became unattainable for his own brothers. And so, the crisis of the Franciscan order already began during Francis's life and continues until today.

Saint Francis did not gather his brothers into conventual communities, whereas monastic centers were created to last. That a fraternity made up of a few brothers tries, even for a generation, to go off to Alverno or Saint-Romain to live, that I can understand. But a fraternity does not ensure continuity.

For us, because of our ecumenical vocation among other things, continuity is necessary. And perhaps also a monastic center, poor in its material appearance, but able to create a climate where human beings maintain their balance.

9. Brother Denis (Jean-Daniel Aubert, 1934–2015), originally from French-speaking Switzerland.

If I love Saint Francis because he reminds us that the Gospel is practiced first and foremost without material support, I am nonetheless convinced that Saint Benedict can inspire us.

There is a humility which consists in not accepting the human gifts one has received; I would call it destructive humility. Our Protestant pessimism, which considers nature as totally fallen, relishes this form of humility: nothing can be considered worthwhile in the order of creation and in creatures!

This destructive humility is a road of anguish; it refuses the peace of Christ.

The call to reconciliation is a language accessible to all. But if we remain with an ecumenism of words, of dialogue, of harmony, of peaceful coexistence, we settle into the inertia of a denominational truce.

Some theologians of ecumenism speak of an "eschatological" ecumenism. If dialogue leads to this conclusion, it was not worthwhile: that would be an ecumenism without hope.

July 13, 1963

Writing and seeking moments of solitude helps me to get a grip on who I am, to be myself. Without solitude, without a dialogue with pen in hand, a dispersion of the inner self takes place.

In a few moments, night prayer. I love to attend. I am so convinced that by remaining before God with my brothers, I allow what is most essential in my life to come to fulfillment. I know this and that is enough.

This movement of human beings towards God in contemplation, prayer, remains full of mystery.

The visit of Don Alfonso Roig plunges me into a universe that is at my door but that I forget—the world of artists. There you find nonconformist attitudes, a sense of wonder, a note of joy, an expectation of new discoveries. I should remember this more often.

I restrict my personal universe too much to the nature around me, the trees, the garden, the sky.

A conversation yesterday with Dominique [10] left a strong impression on me. "Since I have been in Taizé, I have never been bored for a moment," he said. His life is ordered, full, at every moment. For my part, my great temptation is to fill up the empty moments with dialogues. I only find my balance by exercising my energies through intense activity.

I remain astonished that, as I have grown older, it has become possible for me to give lectures and talks without preparing ahead of time. My responsibility makes me a man of words, something not in my nature. To be a man of communication, I have to collect my thoughts, piecing together what I can, setting things out slowly and adding spaces of silence.

During dialogues in my room, I should dare to note things down more often, even if it might seem unconventional. I would like to be able to note down at once certain statements that I am surprised to find myself expressing and that later on I am unable to recall.

Why, moreover, do I have such a halting delivery, sometimes so difficult to follow, when I speak freely to one or another of the brothers? As if I wanted to get rid of what I have to say. It is the same when I write.

Lord, may I become more a man of inwardness.

July 14, 1963

Live to the full this summer in Burgundy. Become more aware of the qualities of this province. Consider it as a whole. I have sometimes been able to be glad at the thought that I was living between

10. Brother Dominique (Gérard Dully, 1938–) from Lausanne, Switzerland. Because of his previous formation as a printer, he was instrumental in setting up the Presses of Taizé and printed books and other works for the community throughout his life. He was also a great lover of insects.

the two great capital cities of Europe that were most alive, Paris and Rome.

This deep-seated sadness that took hold of me three years ago and that has returned so often since then! It makes a great regularity of work and prayer even more indispensable.

Beware of conventions that are contrary to an essential need to live. Throughout my life I have always consented to certain social conventions. I have even imposed them on others. These conventions are my misfortune. I need to analyze them in order to detect them. But then naturally, you can find conventions in everything. Being decently dressed, the refusal to look slovenly, which are so important to me, could be considered a social convention.

July 15, 1963

We are always destined to be incomplete! If our sensitivity to all that comes from our neighbor becomes too intense, the will is dislocated and the personality disintegrates. A person who can no longer make a choice because of his openness is in danger.

We have to accept that we will always be men who aspire to fullness, but whose being is subject to limitations. Knowing how to choose, to cut through indecision and even to cut out certain things, is characteristic of a virile and adult attitude.

The fear of becoming repressed because we cut out some elements, because we curtail our imagination in some areas, would lead to exposing ourselves to another imbalance. There is no repression as long as the choice to make a break is taken in full awareness. It can be maintained afterwards without reflecting, without reasoning.

My immoderate love for the public sphere is sometimes romantic. I do not even manage to remain in contact with the many different trades and professions of all those who live around us in the immediate area.

Suffering rises to the surface in me. Because I am afraid of it, I provoke the things that can trigger it. I returned this evening from the church, at peace. Noticing this peace, I looked for the event which hurt me today, and I found it.

Aware of this inclination, I have to call upon that strength of character which rejects useless worries and moves on to something else. As a matter of fact, I have just done so at this very moment.

It is surprising to realize that, when disturbed by a bad letter, for example, I find peace when I have replied or asked someone to reply, but not before.

The hot weather has come back. The night is warm with stars. And, beneath my window, the sound of the fountain calls to generosity.

July 16, 1963

Inner peace, the peace of Christ: that priceless good without which there is no joy. But does not seeking it and pursuing it mean settling down in a spiritual comfort?

Peace in all things. But who is that complacent man, unable to look at the evil in and around him?

Inner peace is such a great gift that it is worth sacrificing even a little self-satisfaction, provided that, from time to time, we stop to look within, among other things by means of confession conducted by a spiritual father.

Does the joy of forgiveness then fill the heart? Alas, I belong to that generation so allergic to guilt that transgressions and forgiveness are values that have faded. But may I be able to live my life in the peace of forgiveness.

July 17, 1963

The pressure of Protestantism on my mind has caused my vitality to ebb for long periods of time. Moreover, still today when I am intimidated, I lose my voice and have to pull myself together. An absence of vitality that is more psychological than real.

Pierre-Etienne is back from Abidjan.[11] Such an unintimidating brother, and yet, sitting in front of him, I have trouble finding my words. I appreciate the nuances of his judgment and his utter kindheartedness.

The evening meal, in this humid and warm weather, with a colorful sky, a cool dining room, under the lamp a bowl overflowing with red roses—all this set our hearts beating in unison.

This evening the church was full. Are we now heading towards having so many people present, even on weekdays, at this most significant moment of our life?

July 18, 1963

I have just come back from the Church of Reconciliation. In the crypt I glimpsed some young men, sitting at the feet of the icon of the Virgin Mary, singing and praying. This masculine piety is always a tonic for me: virile men bending their knees before the Lord, rooted in a communion with him.

I speak more in terms of peace than of joy. Is that because I am growing older? I realize in any event that joy lies on the road to peace and that the opposite is not true at all.

Some Italian priests from Siena asked me the question: if you had the power (they said: if you were pope), what would you do at once for unity? My answer: let all baptized persons who believe in the real presence receive communion; and secondly, pay great attention to non-believers, open the doors.

Today I have been dreading the iron rule of Rome. How is it, I said to myself, when I know how formidable certain congregations of the Roman curia are, that I can still wish for Christian unity? I should be relieved that we are separated. No, if separation may save us from a trial, the fact of division is a far greater trial still. It

---

11. Pierre Etienne (1922–2011), a French brother who spent years in the fraternities of the community in Africa, notably in Algeria and Niamey (Niger). He published several volumes of poetry.

may possibly have been one of the most constant sufferings of my life.

July 19, 1963

A generous welcome and bread shared are a way of poverty. We are not heading towards security on that road, because we do not know where this hospitality will lead us. But we validate the petition of the Our Father: "Give us this day our daily bread."

July 20, 1963

Anxiety wells up in me and looks for relief in securities. It believes in the assurance given by a house, a place of rest. It does not realize that true rest lies in God alone, in the Christ who dwells within me. The heart needs a strong resolve to keep in check a mind that is errant and anxious. It must be the heart of a mature person, aware that each time we listen to ourselves we find another reason to worry.

July 22, 1963

Among all the different faces of those I have met today, I cannot forget those of the Little Sisters of the Poor. I love them because they have no pretensions. I speak to them about the need to adapt religious life to the contemporary world, about the promotion of women, and they reply that they love one another. Disarmed, all I can do is to pray with them, with a fervent intention for the vocation of religious women. I believe in this so strongly.

Welcome the poorest of the poor. Do everything to manifest a brotherly heart. Do not reject elites, but avoid giving them the best place.

July 24, 1963

A brother asked me the question: what would favor a renewal of Catholic monasticism? I replied: only the ecumenical vocation, looking outwards upon a world coming to birth, and the resolve to set one's prayer and one's life in tune with this vast human reality, the resolve to be open to the present, will make it possible to overcome internal crises. Crises cannot be solved today only by discussing internal reforms. On the contrary, that debate would run the risk of leading to a standstill.

July 26, 1963

Yesterday morning, a choir of young Germans sang in the church. The singing of the final chorale, *O Jesu meine Freude*, reached perfection. For me it is the summit of all choral music. For hours I was nearly overcome.

Preparing for our council occupies me.[12] I have been very concerned about a letter from one of the fraternities[13] informing me of a difficulty that may well have a great impact on our meeting. But my worry diminishes rapidly. I reformulate several points so as to take account of the potential difficulty and, for the last three days, I have noticed that I am being led by God; everything finds its place and acquires a new form. I am a little brother who prays.

12. Once a year, all the brothers in Taizé, and some living in other parts of the world, gather for a few days "in council," to reflect together, review the events of the past year and discuss upcoming projects and events. Over the years it has become less a time of decision-making and more a celebration of community life. See *The Rule of Taizé*, 30–37.

13. After the Second World War, when life in Taizé became less arduous, brothers were sent out across the world in small groups, known as *fraternités*, to live in places of poverty and division, "to be a sign of [Christ's] presence among all people and bearers of joy" (*The Rule of Taizé*, 95).

August 9, 1963

During the time of the council, I have stopped writing in this notebook. A great storm is breaking upon the community, of which it is not aware. I am the only one, or almost, to experience the shocks. I repeat to myself: it is the time to live in peaceful trust in God. He is my rock; I will not falter. At the heart of the sorrow there is nevertheless a peace, that of Christ, my life and my joy. God grants graces; we are inundated with them.

August 10, 1963

Unanimity: one soul. I seek nothing in our life together but this harmony of all around the one thing that matters.

Words repeated as a game create mental attitudes, cause different tendencies to become stronger. In this way the pessimism of discourse enters into our blood.

August 11, 1963

Weariness, struggle. The conflict of not being adapted to the place where we live comes up again and again. Leaving to attend the hundredth anniversary of the Dombes[14] made me nostalgic once again for the countryside of the Bresse on the banks of the Saone River, the vast skies to the west, that hospitable area which is the valley of Macon. The shock on coming back, after the Bois-Clair, as soon as we have to go down into our valley. I know that this is an infantile reaction over which my will has no power. Lord, have mercy.

Discouragement. Yes. But go forward constantly, wiping out unhappiness, borne by Christ, of course. Go forward, do not remain focused on a hardship.

14. The Abbey of Notre-Dame-des-Dombes was a Trappist monastery situated to the southeast of Taizé. For many years it was the site of the *Groupe des Dombes*, which brought together Catholic and Protestant theologians to reflect on ecumenical topics.

August 12, 1963

God's fatherhood is expressed in our lives by having spiritual fathers and by being a spiritual father to others. And the solitude that is part of our human condition is soothed.

Strive at every moment to refuse to follow fleeting thoughts wherever the imagination leads us. Return again and again to the thread of an inner conversation. Call upon an adult mind: a spirit of strength, love and self-control. [15]

The death of Pope John XXIII remains an enduring trial for me. It is the third time of mourning in my adult life. In him a father was given to me, a father who loved all people.

    This need for an entirely loving father is true for every person. In my turn I must not let myself be overly impressed by the contemporary psychological trend that sees paternalism in every expression of spiritual fatherhood. Love my brothers as a true father, be a father for them, always and in everything.

15. 2 Tim 1:7.

1966

There are no journal entries extant for the years 1964 and 1965. The following entries for 1966–1968 are taken from the book Violence des pacifiques (The Violence of Peacemakers), published in 1968, where they intersperse and illustrate Brother Roger's reflections on different topics. Most of them were undated and not placed in chronological order, but rather to correspond to the subjects discussed. We have tried as far as possible to restore them to their original sequence.

In the wake of the Second Vatican Council, Brother Roger's reflections in 1966 focus on the changes brought about by the council and, above all, on the prospects and difficulties of unity between the different Christian traditions. A constant worry of his was that the great impetus made possible by the council would sink into a kind of peaceful coexistence unless concrete steps forward were taken without delay. As he wrote in 1965 in his book Dynamic du provisoire (The Dynamic of the Provisional): "Ecumenism can only make progress if its inner dynamic drives it to become more and more universal. How else could the ecumenical wave slowly but surely gain ground among Christians and, through them, reach all of humanity?"[1]

1. Dynamic of the Provisional, 7.

1966

Know how to wait for opposing tendencies to harmonize: how many times did I repeat this to myself during the Second Vatican Council!

Being plunged into an assembly of that kind constituted a trial of strength. I had prepared myself to deal with it. It is nonetheless the case that I prefer things on a human scale, here in Taizé, sustained by community prayer, rather than being catapulted into a huge gathering, even if it was the most interesting of adventures.

An adventure! We were even more aware of that towards the end. As the closing days approached, tensions grew in parallel with the importance of the decisions. Do we not all harbor the humanly comprehensible wish to see our own tendencies reflected in the documents?

Nothing could be less ecumenical! What has not developed in common cannot be imposed, otherwise we burden others with our own idiosyncracies.

1966

I am happy about the use of modern languages in the liturgy at present, but I know that this is far from enough to prevent mechanical repetition.

I am sometimes wary of Bible readings that are read too quickly during community prayer. There could be in this a kind of magic of words "that have to be read," without being understood. It is not easy for people today to grasp what is read aloud to them. Or am I too harsh, forgetting that some crumbs always fall from the table?

In the church, have there not always been people of the word and people of contemplation? At close hand, a great distance seems to separate them. Seen in perspective, they are nourished by the same bread.

1966

Conversation with some monks. I try to explain our solidarity with them. It is possible that they do not feel at home in our community prayer. And yet we have invented nothing; we have simply adapted the prayer of all the ages.

In any case, everyone gets from it what they can. Our communal prayer is like a mosaic, beautiful for some, shapeless for others. What one person considers meaningless is evocative for another. One appreciates the psalms, or the long silences following the Scripture reading, or the litanies. There are those who especially look forward to the organ music at the end of the service.

To each their crumb. To think that everything could be understood with the same intensity, even by just one person, is utopian.

1966

In Rome, conversation around the dinner table with some theologians considered men of the tradition. The most qualified of them begins to speak about the roads to unity: "If there is sometimes a great gap between Catholic and Protestant theological schools, there are equally deep divisions between different Catholic theological tendencies. The difference between Thomism and the Franciscan or Augustinian schools is just as great as that between Luther and Saint Thomas Aquinas." It is thus possible to hope: if they agree to be complementary, different orientations can coexist in true unity, not just between East and West, but among Western Christians themselves.

June 1966

I have never before had so many dialogues with unbelievers. Again yesterday one of them, a man of letters whom I have not yet met, dedicated his last book to me with the words: "Hoping that your openness can welcome an agnostic."

And then a few days ago, during the many sessions that take place right here, two young students from our region, both unbaptized, came to tell me of their upcoming marriage. They are not going to ask for a blessing. That would be dishonest, they said. The girl belongs to a family in which, for several generations, perhaps since the revolution, no one has ever been baptized. He too comes from a non-Christian family.

But the festive day of their wedding should be marked by an event, they feel. Why not a time of sharing in which the two families would take part? So, on the evening of the wedding I meet with these families, of solid stock, in our church. We share a few words. Our dialogue was possible because one man, John XXIII, had set things in motion. We told one another that.

June 1966

Some brothers and I have gone for a few days of rest in a house with a terrace that overlooks the sea. What could be more appealing! The air always in motion, the sea breezes, the fragrances, the clear light of morning and the waning of the heat every evening, after the torpor of the day.

At that hour irresistibly I escape, for a few moments, to the west terrace, near two orange trees. A time of reflection. This evening I realize how burdensome the last two years have been. So many times when I could not see how I would be able to undertake the next efforts which, in fact, I always do manage to accomplish when the time comes. That was not my experience during the first twenty-five years at Taizé.

A conviction passes through my mind: this huge battle to be waged is with the powers of a world of darkness. Those powers do not want Christian unity. They know that Christ is in agony in the face of his people torn apart. And so I have accepted that the struggle may well become even more intense.

Calmed down, I still have to master the possible weariness. To do all I can to get through the bad days. There is no other way out than to cast myself into Christ. Call upon him at every occasion, know that he is near. The meal this evening was illuminated by this. No one could have been aware of it, but I was a man rich with the friendship of Christ and of his brothers.

July 1966

These days, the presence among us of the spiritual families of Charles de Foucauld[2] has offered us an occasion to take stock of the friendship that has always united us. Had the unity of the church been a reality at the beginning of Taizé, we would not have hesitated: Father de Foucauld's family corresponded to what we were looking for at that time. But, on account of the ecumenical vocation, our ways parted. At a certain moment, we had to leave our silence to offer hospitality, to young people in particular.

Moreover, in the early days of our community, a woman[3] expressed her strong conviction that sending all the brothers out in small groups would contradict the visible sign of community which would be a point of reference for Christians. In a world where everything incites to dispersion, this sign remains essential. Perhaps she already glimpsed the conditions of contemporary life that are dislocating societies and individuals, impelling them to spend moments of intensity with a community.

Summer 1966

I spent what may well turn out to have been the most momentous evening of the year. I received some friends from Poland. The conversation went along peacefully until I heard them say: in the great difficulties of their existence, in the balance they are trying to maintain between the Marxists and the institutional church, they

2. See note 25, page 43.

3. It was Madame Boegner, the wife of Marc Boegner (1881–1970), French pastor and theologian, longtime president of the Protestant Federation of France and member of the Académie Française.

constantly refer to a small community that is contemporary with them and that sustains their hope.

Hearing such a powerful statement referring to oneself causes surprise and unease. And still, I am not writing down everything they said. I was led to address all my brothers, together in council, to say to them:

Who are we? A gathering of men who did not choose one another and who are trying to relive something of the first Christian community.

Who are we? A community that is small and fragile, sustained by a preposterous hope, the reconciliation of Christians and of all humanity; a community of Christians asked to accomplish tasks too great for them but who, in spite of their small number, try to respond to calls coming from everywhere.

Nothing would happen if we were not first and foremost a community of men who persevere, each within himself, in a struggle which can be very arduous, for Christ and for him alone.

One day, the pride of life can insinuate itself into us. What was purely the response to a call is dissolved. The void is then filled by something else—a need for power, a kind of personal triumphalism, hostility towards what represents the original call, either from within or without.

Perseverance! That is one of the inner themes that find a resonance each day, at a time in history when more and more things are called into question. We cannot remain faithful by means of continuous fireworks. They would blind us and keep us from living in reality. If it is good that, from time to time, one of these fireworks comes to bring us joy, that helps us to return to perseverance, tirelessly.

So who are we? A tiny community, sometimes shaken to the foundations. But it always gets up again because it is led onward by a presence that is beyond it and that links it to eternity.

Who are we? If I had to sum up our present situation in a few words: we are a kind of accumulation of individual weaknesses, but a community visited by Someone other than ourselves.

1966

A few days ago, after having replied to questions from a group of over thirty nations, I wanted in turn to ask them how they saw us. They thought about it. This is what they said: is it right to discern in your community on the one hand a vocation to suffering, and on the other a Gospel freshness? If so, all we can say is: remain who you are.

1966

Tedious conversation. Someone wants to know what is specific about Protestantism as opposed to Catholicism. I take my courage in hand to answer him, even though a voice in my head says to me: change the subject!

More than three hundred Protestant denominations: you would have to be an expert to orient yourself! What is specific about Protestantism? To simplify, I reply only on the basis of our own life here.

One of our brothers, from a Protestant church in the north of Europe, never saw the Eucharist with the celebrant facing the people before coming here. Another learnt, as a child, to make the sign of the cross. Still another practiced confession and received absolution. Another brother, also a Protestant, saw the Eucharist celebrated with the old vestments—chasuble, stole, crozier and miter for the bishop, candles before the crucifix and on the altar. In his church, bread was never used but only hosts. Yet another, more exceptionally, was taught by his father, a pastor, to venerate the Virgin Mary.

If you look at the diversity of Protestantism, none of those things are specific to it, but all of them belongs to it. So where does the dividing-line fall? The crucial point remains doubtlessly the refusal of the ministry of the pope and the recent dogmas concerning the Virgin Mary.

I often think about the inner dialogue I had with myself when I was young and rediscovered the faith. I found it hard to understand certain people's statements regarding the Lord's Supper. For some, it was merely a matter of coming together to recall Christ. Others only saw a fraternal meal.

Formed by Scripture since I was a child, I compared two sayings. The first: "When two or three are gathered in my name, I am there in their midst."[4] The second: "This is my body; this is my blood."[5] I said to myself: If I am together with other Christians, he is present. He promised it, and I take him at his word. But if I receive the bread and wine of the Eucharist, that is another presence; I am incorporated into the Risen Christ. Otherwise what is the point of that meal?

In saying "This is my body," Christ speaks of a presence which is quite different than the spiritual presence he promised to two or three gathered in his name.

Rooting our lives in the real presence of Christ in the Eucharist means relying on a faith which does not belong to us. Rejecting it might possibly dispose people to understand us better, but where then would the Gospel be?

1966

A friend asks me, "You are a realist. Why, then, in your writings, is there no negative evaluation or criticism, either with regard to Protestantism or to Catholicism?"

"Don't ever forget," I replied, "that just recently we have emerged from an old history made up of centuries of incomprehension. A sensibility was created; mental processes were set in motion. So many reciprocal judgments were made between Christians of different denominations. None of them have led to a conversion of outlook in the others, nor did they foster the desired changes."

Regarding this or that question addressed to the Catholic Church, responses are in the process of taking shape. But it is up to

4. Matt 18:20.
5. Matt 26:26–29.

the Catholic Church to formulate them from within. In the situation where we find ourselves now, protesting in order to cause the other side to come back to the road that seems best to us can only lead to greater rigidity instead of opening things up.

Personally, my deepest wish is never to cast anathemas on anyone. That does not mean consenting to an error, but speaking out at the right moment. There is a pedagogy of discretion that animates the forces of life within us. People only truly become themselves in an atmosphere of trust. Through trust alone can everything be said.

A welcome extended with unlimited kindness makes it possible for dialogue to ripen one day into sharing. Begun among Christians, it can be widened to include agnostics or non-believers.

1966

The same question keeps coming back: with a view to unity, what would you like to see change in Protestantism and Catholicism? How to reply, without judging from one's own serene heights?

To see many Protestants renounce intolerance, that aberration of Christianity. Protestantism produced intolerance to defend itself. The result is a need to segregate. The temptation to pull up the wheat with the weeds[6] leads to an unconscious and secret complacency. It leads, strange as it may seem, to a triumphalism of the small group, as a Reformed pastor, a kind and peaceful man, told me after a Protestant assembly.

As for Catholics, can we hope that many will free themselves from a need for power, or even at times for domination? This need still characterizes some church institutions. Far from fostering creativity, it is a dead weight.

6. See Matt 13:24–30.

1966

Each day has its own struggle, as every committed person knows. Otherwise, it is impossible to go forward. But for everyone, the capacity to make decisions is renewed until death. The energy of the will is constantly reborn; its resources are inexhaustible and undreamed of.

Often I look back at the lost opportunities, all the places where it would have been good to found the community, and I compare those situations with our region near Macon, so poor in human terms, debilitated as far as the church is concerned.

Living in the past or the future is pointless. The imagination dramatizes things. Only today matters. Nobody can live without looking forward to a certain extent, but anticipating is deadly.

October 1966

These years when we are living through a long-term war, how deeply we were affected, during a night prayer, to hear a Vietnamese man passing through Taizé pronounce these words[7]:

> I am afraid of my fear,
> I am afraid of leaving you, Lord.
> I am afraid of my fear.
> I am afraid I will not hold out till the end.
> Do not forget that I live for you.
> Give me the grace to give my whole life
> And the love that will make me one with you.

1965—1966?

Visit to parishes in a large city in the South of Italy. We were in contact with a university parish, too.

---

7. That monk, the prior of the Benedictine monastery of Hué, returned to his country. He died during the last years of the Vietnam War, the victim of a particularly cruel torture.

On Sunday morning, all the churches were filled to overflowing. An evident participation in Italian, a sermon rooted in Scripture. Is the suspiciousness of some people—and I include myself at times among them—regarding the regions of Christendom justified? When the wind of the Holy Spirit blows, and this is evidently the case in the renewals underway, it is not unusual to see the laity of an entire area, whose religion had previously been little more than a formality, become enthusiastic about what they are discovering.

On the other hand, in places where everything has disappeared, as for example in our own region, no one really sees the full meaning of the tireless generosity of pastors and a few lay people, who live in a kind of desert. Around them, there is no resonance to the witness of their lives. How much patience is needed to see these arid lands blossom once again!

1966?

A priest I have never met wrote me a letter. I have fixed a copy of it on the wall of my room. For years now, I stop and read it from time to time:

"Today is the tenth anniversary of my ordination and I cannot keep from thinking of you and of your community. Together, we are climbing by different paths that mountain which is Christ.

"I thought of a little shortcut that could enable us to come together more quickly. That little way is spiritual childhood.

"I firmly believe that this is how unity will be achieved. An ultimate union will be able to come about in a climate of spiritual childhood, in other words humility, simplicity, trust, and surrender.

"That is a path, a track, that I point out in all humility and simplicity."

1966–1967?

A pastor asks me what has caused us the most suffering. The hardest thing has been the intolerance, particularly coming from our own churches.[8] Why, from the beginning, this refusal to consider as a vocation a yes pronounced for life in response to a call? After a silence of more than four centuries following the Reformation, we wished to live in celibacy. But how many times did we have to hear this argument: you cannot imprison the freedom of the Holy Spirit by a lifetime commitment.

In the early years, we renewed our yes to celibacy year after year. Then we realized that the Holy Spirit was strong enough to bind for life men who, on account of Christ, wanted to remain permanently in the state in which they were found when they were called.[9]

At first, we were far from realizing how relevant this gift was. Much later we discovered in it an exercise of openness to all people.

I should add here a fact that has meaning for me. Shortly before my first communion, I had tried to convince my father, a pastor, to postpone the date. But he could not risk being reproached for having a son who did not comply with an obligation that nobody else refused. At Easter, all the boys and girls of sixteen, without exception, made their first communion. In the end I had to go along with his thinking. I thought that he was assuming his responsibility and I preferred to ignore its cost to myself. The day of my first communion, my father gave me this Gospel text: "Be faithful until death, and I will give you the crown of life."[10] Only much later did I pay attention to it. Perhaps that living Word did not return to God empty.[11]

---

8. When these lines were written, the community was made up of brothers from different Protestant backgrounds. There were not yet any Catholic brothers.

9. See 1 Cor 7:20.

10. Rev 2:10.

11. See Isa 55:10–11.

Undated

While I am conversing with a group of lay people, a brusque voice shouts out: can prayer be anything else than a monologue with oneself? After a few seconds of silence, I dare to reply:

In communicating with God, a person begins a dialogue not with himself, but in himself. What characterizes this dialogue is that the person continues it while remaining consciously in God's presence. Is he always aware of that presence? There are times when it is not at all perceptible. We are then in a state of pure faith, with no outward support; we walk forward in the dark.

The dialogue within oneself continues. It is a poor exchange. But at the end of a long period, moments arise when a presence gently makes itself felt. So God's silence was not at all detrimental.

It is true that some people get lost in discussions with themselves. They think they are meditating. They are obviously living in the illusion of a dialogue.

1966?

Reflecting on the encounter with Christ on the last day, that meeting of which I am not at all afraid, I found myself writing: what will I be asked in that first conversation about which I know very little, except that it will be the first of many, for all eternity?

Perhaps some people are right to say that any attempt to represent ultimate realities is premature. Still, I tried to answer and I imagined the dialogue. Will I not hear myself saying:

...as for the community, what I loved about it was something that many people would not even think of. They appreciate Taizé for its openness, for the dialogue with so many different people. More than that sharing, I considered contemplative waiting to be the most important thing.

You have suffered. You have also wished to live the Gospel's call to chastity. You have tried to be, in the midst of humanity and for it, signs of the timeless, signs to be invented and brought to life over and over again each day. This waiting was situated beyond gifts of the intelligence. It was made possible for each brother, even the one who felt he was the most disadvantaged. That was what was most powerful.

Yes, the main thing was the struggle within, lived in a daily re-creation.

1967

The year 1967 was marked by the beginnings of the vast social changes that would explode in 1968, notably among the younger generations and the poor of the earth. This was already sensed by the Taizé brothers living on other continents, especially in Recife (Brazil) and Chicago (USA). Brother Roger's own contacts with young people grew, and he noticed their increasing disillusionment with church institutions. At the same time, the question of faithfulness to a religious or priestly vocation took on more importance at a time when many were abandoning their commitment in the wake of the upheavals occasioned by the Council.

Early 1967

A young brother, just catapulted into a slum in Recife, in the Northeast of Brazil, where no one knows what tomorrow will bring, wrote to me: "In the face of all you can see, a constant striving for balance is necessary to calm the reactions caused by injustice. There are questions you ask yourself: if God exists, why is there evil? If God is good, why is there suffering? If God is good and all-powerful, why is there humiliation and hatred? No definitive explanation. You have to look for a living answer."

Another young brother, back from a fraternity, spoke to me of the apparent uselessness of being immersed in the heart of Chicago, in the ghetto of colored people. What can a few Christians, with no means of effectiveness, accomplish in these huge contemporary societies that are so well organized, running frantically after profit? And now two brothers who have just returned from Africa tell the same story.

June 1967

Learned from our Franciscan brothers[1] the details of Paul VI's welcome to the chapter of their order. After reading out a message, the pope addressed them spontaneously and said: "Your road, one which is far from unknown to the younger generation with their unconventional tastes, is the road of non-conformity."[2] That a pope called upon Catholics to be non-conformists should be a cause for rejoicing in many Protestant families: they fought hard to remain faithful to that attitude.

But as soon as non-conformity becomes a system, the worst kind of misunderstanding arises. A non-conformist attitude requires constant revision. People are quickly satisfied with paying

1. Between 1964 and 1972, a small fraternity of Franciscan friars lived in Taizé alongside the brothers, at a time when it was not yet possible for Catholics to be part of the community.

2. "Discorso di Paolo VI al capitolo generale dell'ordine dei Frati Minori." June 22, 1967. http://www.vatican.va/content/paul-vi/it/speeches/1967/june/documents/hf_p-vi_spe_19670622_frati-minori.html.

lip-service to a position, and this keeps them from putting it into practice.

Summer 1967

At the entrance to our church I often spend a few moments before the community prayer speaking with those who come for the service. This evening I listened to some young people marked by violence against church institutions. They demand immediate action and are hard on the church, where they see only death and ruin. If they cannot see the face of God in Christians, then they can no longer believe in the church.

Some of them, in order to make it easier to encounter others, have relativized the content of the faith. For them everything can be called into question, as long as people get along. For these young people, communion with God is an abstraction.

Confronted with this shaking of the foundations, all during the liturgy, in the peace of the common prayer, tears flowed within me. And in a dream, I was surprised to find myself looking forward to death, whereas from morning till night I marvel at the gift of life.

1967

It is late at night. I am thinking over what some young people told me today. I can see in my mind some of their faces, the clear but troubled eyes of a very young girl. I can still hear the harsh but serious voice of a boy who was criticizing the church.

Undeniably their revolt springs from a legitimate suffering at the inconsistency of this or that church institution. But I sense with all my being the turmoil that this violence will cause.

It is true that, for two thousand years now, people have been speaking about the end of Christianity. On the eve of the year 1000, at the Renaissance, at the Enlightenment, large numbers of people were convinced of it.

1967

A young brother pointed out to me to what extent our life at Taizé requires us to pay attention to a whole host of different factors. How right he is!

Our position constantly situates us at the heart of serious tensions. To foster unity in the Body of Christ, we have to listen to aspirations that vary according to nationalities or early training. This necessity keeps us, I hope, from taking up partisan positions.

Today, at the little council that brings us all together on some evenings, I commented the text: giving one's entire life for Christ.[3] And I said to my brothers: during our daily meetings I do not speak about trials, about this or that unfounded statement that is made about us and to which we do not reply in order to avoid polemics. I say nothing about what causes us to suffer. Why this silence? Why instead do I only mention what encourages us? For fear of placing a stumbling-block on someone's path. And yet, just this morning, how many times did I repeat to myself: unless the grain of wheat dies . . .[4]

September 1967

For our part, we have been discovering in recent years that systematic desacralization dissolves of its own accord when young people attend community prayers. Even during a gathering of 1,600 young people, they rushed to take part in the community prayer three times a day.[5] A continuous prayer went on throughout the night in the crypt of the church. There too, many of them were present.

Why do they come to pray with us? Many react positively when they come to know that a number of my brothers are called to undertake a challenging way of life in the working world. In

3. Cf. Matt 16:25.

4. John 12:24.

5. The second ecumenical gathering of young adults took place in Taizé from August 31 to September 3, 1967.

their turn, it is also in an impossible situation, amidst the indifference of so many, that these young people will have to persevere.

1967

At my table, an old friend, a Protestant layman of rare open-mindedness. He tells me that one of his pupils is going to marry a man who has left his religious order after twelve years of community life. Then the conversation moves on to other things. But I am frozen with heartache. Our sentiments cannot correspond; he is a man responsible for his teaching, and I am the brother of my brothers.

What would I not give up in order to help men to reflect on their initial decision and to rediscover a way of being faithful until death to a commitment they have made?

Attentive to welcoming those who are in difficulty, at certain times in my life I have given the priority to outside visitors, even to the extent of neglecting personal conversations with my brothers. And yet such dialogues are essential; through them our outlooks gradually come to change.

In Chicago, the fraternity where some of my brothers live together with a few Franciscans has the same concern. Lacking space in their house to welcome others, they rented an additional apartment. Why? Only to offer hospitality to priests and religious who have broken with their vocation. By allowing them to stay with them for a few days, they hope they can help them to reflect.

During the Second Vatican Council, I abruptly realized that the unity of the Catholic Church would survive all the reforms, except in one case. The church would break in half if priests already committed to celibacy were authorized to marry. After a thousand years in which the priesthood and celibacy have been intimately linked, it would be like touching a raw nerve. The Catholic faithful are not prepared for such a change.

And yet, no one can be unaware that, in certain regions, chastity is sometimes impossible for priests who are isolated, even if they are on fire with a pastoral vocation. How often am I surprised to find myself thinking of those men!

1967

Poignant conversation with a priest who is a friend of ours. He thinks he is supporting a religious brother by helping him leave his congregation. He feels that it is already dead. And yet 2,500 men are still members of it.

I explain to him the drama of the Reformation. At a certain moment, despair at not seeing reforms arising within Catholicism gained the upper hand. People chose to set out without all their brothers and sisters. God allowed his Spirit to breathe on this new creation: he loves his people too much to abandon them. But the image of the unity of Christ's body faded.

A few days ago, another priest assured me that the monastery where he spent some time had no future. And yet, when institutions are exhausted, it is still possible to count on the men and women who animate them. In this particular case I am convinced, since I know him, that the man in charge of that monastery is capable of reawakening his whole community.

Every transformation in a person begins inwardly. Our mental structures change from within. It is in the depths of our being that a continual conversion to Christ, who is constantly forgotten and refused, takes place.

Of course every effort needs to be made to reform age-old structures. But if they are not animated by men and women of generosity, reforms may give them a fine appearance, they will have the distinction of an inner logic, but they will not shed any light.

October 28, 1967

When Pope Paul VI went first to meet Patriarch Athenagoras,[6] he used his authority to set things in motion once again. And when the same Paul VI spoke to the church of Constantinople as to a sister-church, with a single word he brought ecclesiology out of an impasse. The Bishop of Rome does not wait passively; he takes the initiative. Without a recognized authority, his acts would be short-lived.

I was present this morning, in Rome, at their third meeting: Patriarch Athenagoras was welcomed in St. Peter's.

Behind us, a Greek woman was making a fuss. She felt she had been given a bad place and made no bones about it. Her seat was not in keeping with the dignity of her church.

In front of us, a large podium on which two identical armchairs were set facing each other, one for the pope, the other for the patriarch. I was overjoyed at Paul VI's intention to place Athenagoras beside him in this way. The Orthodox will be sensitive to this gesture.

The prayer begins, then come the speeches. As the minutes pass, the more the silhouette of Paul VI seems to blend into the shadow of the venerable patriarch. And then a question comes to my mind. What if, with a view to reaching unity, the idea of a two-headed church seemed to be a necessary way forward? But then it would no longer be in the image of the body. It would lead, as a result, to a kind of federalism.

1967

A friend asks me: could my entire life as a Christian be based on a wager? I reply: we live surrounded by people who have abandoned the faith. Because of them we can no longer translate our conviction into the language of yesterday; we would wear out those

6. Pope Paul VI and Patriarch Athenagoras of Constantinople met three times: in the Holy Land in 1964, in Istanbul in 1967 and in Rome in October of that same year.

who are living in a kind of Holy Saturday, the day when God was dead. But this conviction of ours, expressed in a new language, is not based on a wager. It is founded on the testimony of witnesses whose honesty is beyond all doubt. In saying this, I was thinking of another man who is very dear to me. Involved in organizing and trade-union work, he has a skeptical temperament. One day he told me about a visit from Christ: a living word heard in solitude at a time he least expected it! How could his faith—and mine in consequence—be based on a wager?

1967

Dialogue with a brother leaving for a fraternity. What are we to be? A living word at the heart of injustice and segregation; a prayer, through an existence which is absurd, rationally speaking; a language spoken to God, by everything done for and with the least fortunate; a page on which every new suffering endured for his Body, the Church, is being written down.[7]

Recently, a religious brother protested against the presence of one of our fraternities, because our brothers refused to take the same positions as he did. The man who writes is an intellectual. He knows how to wield a pen. He wants us as well to take a stand by writing. It would be enough to sign this or that document and we would be men who have made a commitment. Committed to what, exactly?

The fact of experiencing, day after day, the wounds of a humdrum existence, sharing the conditions of women and men without hope, is a form of commitment that is more costly than signing petitions or writing texts, however just they might be.

I know that at times manifestos have produced a shock-effect and have committed those who engaged themselves in that way. But at present they are all-pervasive, to say the least. So many people are asked to sign texts, to take sides for or against. Is it not more constructive to be people who listen? This attitude has never kept

7. Col 1:24.

us from taking part in the life of society. For those of my brothers who have lived or who are living the condition of workers, for those who are immersed in the life of the poorest, their presence means taking a stand. It does not require manifestos. Sometimes such texts do not commit us to anything; they soothe the conscience and nothing more.

Drafting praiseworthy resolutions at the end of a meeting can lead to hypocrisy. We affirm something in writing, we condemn, we issue warnings, and that changes nothing in our lives. This process is becoming one of the sicknesses of our day.

1967–1968?

Some theology students affirm that they can no longer keep going within the present structures. They ask me what can be created to find a way out of a blind alley.

I look at these young men. One of them, Pierre, seems the personification of a well-balanced individual. In another, I sense a deep disillusionment.

I try to reply. It is only possible to weather a crisis in the context in which it has found us. If we run away from a momentary trial to create something else, we lose an ability to adapt.

1967–1968

Letters from two of my brothers, received practically at the same time, are significant. One is from Brazil, the other from the United States.

From Recife: "Life in the midst of people who are among the poorest on the planet has its moments of fullness. The harshness of the unemployment that affects us, because our European nationalities and our culture make us suspect in the factories, is compensated for by the hospitality. A family is capable of giving a stranger all the food in their shack, even if this means going without eating for a few days.

"In Brazil art reaches a high level of expression, a result of the mixing of cultures and races. The *bossa nova* in poetry, song, and literature has a universal appeal. It will have an impact, for Western nations, similar to the African contribution of jazz."

From Chicago: "Our friends, the Blacks among whom we live, are gradually separating from liberal-minded whites. Among our friends there are four black pastors, and three of them said: We want black power, so go to the whites and teach them whatever you want.

"So many young people ask us: where is hope? The risen Christ. I don't know how else to answer.

"In our fraternity, now that some refuse our friendship, what else can we do but pray on our knees: Christ, have mercy on us, for we are white?"

It is true that two black men are living with them and sharing their heartache.

A newspaper photograph came with the letter. It shows a battle between young people, Asian, white, and black, in the street where our brothers live.

1967?

Anyone who has to exercise authority knows well that there is a reality he has to take into account—the harshness of being judged and humiliated.

People are more or less humiliated according to whether they take risks or not: every courageous step taken involves being criticized.

Too many repeated humiliations can lead to becoming worn-out. And then even the person most deeply rooted in Christ is tempted to look for compensations on a psychological level.[8] They are often found in the vanity of honors or defending one's choices in a certain way. Such a person can be led to exalt his or her ego without realizing it.

8. Brother Roger uses the word "psychic" here. See note 5 for June 25, 1954.

And yet even if a person leaves behind a vast written body of work, what impact will they have had? At most they will influence a few small groups. In the world of the churches, those who are most appreciated are admired by only a limited number of people. There are very few exceptions. Why then this need to stand out? If we look closely, we see that only a few admirers are necessary to keep a destructive fire burning. All the churches are subject to this defect.

Another form of compensation is violence against the people who have humiliated them. Anyone who succumbs to this slides into misery. They see accusations everywhere and sink into darkness. They forget that "happy are the peacemakers."[9]

There are days when you want to cry out: stop this war with yourself; seek compensations only in God's goodness and in a few trustworthy friends.

Is it not required of every person, even the one most subject to humiliation, to take up his cross each morning without showing those around them that he is bearing it?

1967?

On the topic of friendship, I wrote to one of my brothers:

"Friendship is an incalculable value. Generally we grasp only its outlines. We reach the depths only at rare moments.

"Through the dialogue which it makes possible and in serene openness we discover, by no means all, but a few fragments of our being. In this way a creation takes shape in us, tending towards a kind of new birth in Christ."

A brother wrote to me in turn:

"At those times when God tests us to ascertain our degree of friendship with him, our friendships with other human beings and with our brothers take on a dimension of eternity."

9. Matt 5:9.

Undated

Some notes on a sermon by an Anglican bishop in our church:

—We talk too often of love and people do not understand. They would understand better if we spoke of friendship.

—Friendship requires trust. In religious terms, we call this faith.

—Friendship also implies conversation. In religious terms, this is known as prayer.

—Friendship is expressed by gestures—shaking hands, embracing. They are signs of it. In religious terms, these are the sacraments."

And the bishop concluded: "Friendship of whatever sort always involves an element of adoration."

1968

1968 was a symbolic year for the Western world. Revolution was in the air. Student demonstrations broke out in many countries; in France they led to a general strike in May and a virtual shutdown of the country for a time. In the United States, Martin Luther King was assassinated, leading to racial violence. The Vietnam War continued to incite protests and divisions. The situation in Latin America remained tense. All of this found echoes in Brother Roger's journals, but he also found time to reflect on prayer and the inner life.

February 1968

Conversation with twenty young West Berliners. Of Protestant background, they display their skepticism regarding all church institutions. Only violence interests them. They have been deeply affected by the death of one of their comrades, killed by the police during a demonstration. They ask me: why does your community refuse to use the press to influence public opinion? You are known in Germany and you could do a lot. Why do you yourself, as prior, not speak out more? I reply:

—All the brothers complement one another, I as much as the rest.

—But it is up to you to speak. You are unaware of the audience you have.

—What matters is what is inside a person. The outward image that some people may have is of little concern to me. And that inner man prefers a certain silence; he has little faith in declarations.

—You should write to the President of the United States.

—I already have, and I have no illusions about the effect of my letter. Moreover, many people have spoken out and the Vietnam War has not ceased for all that.

—So only violence is effective.

—Violence is the answer only if every means of passive resistance and persuasion have been tried. It is not possible to take such extreme measures without a spirit purified of all self-interest. And we must remember: "Whoever lives by the sword will die by the sword."[1]

I advise them to read this very evening a passage from a recent thought-provoking document on "the development of peoples." I insist on the fact that, for the first time, a pope, after having warned against the temptation of violence, has shown in writing an understanding that it may break out in exceptional situations, "where there is manifest, longstanding tyranny which would do

---

1. Matt 26:52.

great damage to fundamental personal rights and dangerous harm to the common good of the country."[2]

Why are these young people here asking me questions? The topic of ecumenism holds no interest for them. Being Protestant or Catholic scarcely matters to them. They do not know where they stand with regard to their faith. We are all the more surprised to see them take communion during our daily Eucharist.

Back alone in my room, I have the feeling I cannot let them leave without listening to them one more time. There is a prophetic quality in their violence and I cannot shut my ears. I remember that as he died, Jesus promised eternal life to a man of violence.[3]

The last day, I invite them to come to the house for breakfast. I notice the steely gaze of a girl, animated by an icy passion. She has the power to create a kind of unanimity on the necessity of violence. If a psychiatrist were present, he would have spoken of group psychosis. It is true that some of the prophets of the Bible were far from possessing a total psychological balance! Fortunately these young men and women, receiving explosive arguments smack in the face as I have, have been able to think the questions through again with an admirable authenticity.

The Vietnam War is intolerable for them. They want to act. I reply: personally I would like one of my brothers to go to Vietnam with a young American who is now at Taizé and deeply wounded inwardly by the war. For your part, what could you do?

The girl leading the group speaks of Latin America. We should bring revolution there to liberate the poor. We should create other Vietnams, in Christian circles and elsewhere.

I answer that it may still be possible to find solutions without starting a bloody revolt. Women and children do not ask to be victims of that.

For you, what matters is getting involved. So finish your studies quickly; a minimum of preparation is indispensable as a prerequisite.

2. Encyclical letter *Populorum progressio* by Pope Paul VI (March 26, 1967), §31.

3. See Luke 23:43.

Once you are involved, perhaps some of you will come, in conscience, to the point of an attitude of insurrection against manifest, longstanding tyranny that oppresses the human person and has no respect for life. At that moment, it will be important once again to examine your deepest motivations. The temptation of violence is in us all, our whole life long. If it leads to the conviction that we have to destroy in order to rebuild afterwards, the first thing to do is to ask oneself questions.

When you identify violence with destruction, could you be fanatics with a fixed idea? Are there not some who cherish the secret hope of becoming political leaders? The arguments may be lofty, while the real motivation is not. It is not free of ulterior motives, still less is it really selfless.

Destructive violence runs the risk of undergoing a series of escalations. The more liberal-minded are decapitated by the second or third wave, because they refuse destruction as an end in itself.

It is true that in Latin America our cross as Christians is the image projected by this or that person who wears a Christian label. Contempt for the humanity of the poor, the use of power, in other words violence in disguise, what a face of the church! Newspapers and television do not fail to transmit the spectacle.

The need for power through money is a form of tyranny. But it can also be exercised without money. There are police states where capitalism is disappearing or has disappeared. And what an oppressive means of power! Tyranny can be nourished by the most humanitarian of theories and, underneath the fine ideas, conceal the worst state of human enslavement.

****

Yesterday the Berliners. Today, though we are out in the countryside and it is the middle of winter, I find myself dealing with the same topics. Young people from another European country ask me the same questions. Straightaway I sense a bitterness. It was not present in the Berliners.

In a word they ask me: why do you refuse to destroy church institutions? You should make it your business to do away with them. Without violence we will get nothing from the hierarchy. We would prefer that your community had never existed if it does not come to share this outlook.

I try to understand. In the dialogue that begins, I recall saying, among other things: are you conscious of your own motives? Are you able to call yourself into question as well? Do you reflect on the patience (patience means suffering) needed for every creative undertaking, in every birth-process?

1968

At Taizé, we have made use of violence in the face of a Christian conscience that is hardened by denominational separations and that has made its peace with divisions. Our violence, restrained of course, looked for a language to shout out our indignation. In community prayer, in singing the psalms, it found an expression and a way of being activated, incomparably.

April 5, 1968

This morning, as I was leaving community prayer, a brother whispered in my ear, "Martin Luther King has been assassinated."

The death of a friend is costly, especially for my brothers in Chicago. Where will armed violence lead us, when it kills the best?

I dread to think what will happen to the Blacks without their prophet.

He was the bearer of a word. He wanted non-violence. Since that expression has been invented, we have to use it. But it is not ideal. Every human being has violence within them, including Martin Luther King. But the use he made of it was so selfless that in him Another was visible.

The violence of peacemakers breaks the chain reactions of the powerful of our day, the reactions that camouflage an intolerable violence, the domination of the poor. By the gift of his life for his friends,[4] Martin Luther King opens a way for us. No one will have the power to shut it again.

This way is perilous. And he knew it: "I have been battered by the storms of persecution. I must admit that at times I have felt that I could no longer bear such a heavy burden. [. . .] I have learned now that the Master's burden is light precisely when we take his yoke upon us."[5]

His death leads me to look for a meaning in my own death. If a person cannot give a meaning to his death, he cannot really live either.[6]

Some undergo a brutal death. Others lose their life bit by bit; they are underfed, unemployed. There are also those who, by their responsibility for a family, experience a slow death: they have to assume in their flesh the bitterness of close relatives.

May 1968

These days, most of the country has been shut down by strikes.

The situation pains us deeply. When it began, we felt we were out in the wilderness because we were not directly involved in the events. Gradually I became aware of the authenticity of an entire lifetime spent in the presence of God to deepen a search for justice within. What suggestion could I make in this respect to my brothers here? Could some of them leave Taizé each day to work in factories? It is true that some of us are present among

---

4. See John 15:13.

5. https://kinginstitute.stanford.edu/king-papers/documents/suffering -and-faith#fn3.

6 These words make it hard not to think of the circumstances when, at the age of 90, Brother Roger was killed in the Church of Reconciliation during evening prayer by a deranged woman. Naturally, the very idea of desiring a violent death would never have entered his mind. But as the prior of the Grande Chartreuse wrote on that occasion, "The dramatic circumstances of Brother Roger's death are nothing but an outer covering making yet clearer his vulnerability, something that he cultivated as a preferred doorway through which God can come and enter us."

the poorest of the poor on other continents, sometimes as workers. And for the last twelve years, at Taizé, one of our brothers has been collaborating with local people in development projects. His work has already led to harsh oppositions from without. Do we have the strength, in this place of reconciliation, to run the risk of additional misunderstandings from those outside the community?

I asked some of these questions to young couples with whom I frequently meet to try and review our lives. They were surprised to hear me say that their remarks are meaningful for the ongoing journey of our community. They have no idea of the result of our conversations for our own life. Are we not all in the same boat? We find it so hard to believe what we represent for others.

Afterwards we spoke of one of their main concerns. Has the time not come, for them, to look for another way of living, to form a fraternity of households? Living in the same conditions as everyone else their sharing, as complete as possible, their prayer together, would commit them to a brand-new lifestyle. We would be able to rely on them, and vice versa.

June 1968

The students are demonstrating in Paris. I receive a message including these lines: "Will you please pray for us? We feel terribly alone and lost. We got ourselves beaten up out of solidarity and now we have woken up to the fact that we have been manipulated on all sides, by ourselves as much as by others. It's impossible to understand anything. We are still too dazed by what has happened to be able really to analyze it while we are in the midst of it. Talking about it seems useless. As for praying, there are times when that is no longer possible."

During the demonstrations in the universities, some of the students have been coming to Taizé to share. Different tendencies emerge. The great majority reflect with a seriousness characteristic of the younger generations. Some have lost weight. An inner fire burns within them.

On three occasions I met a student from the Sorbonne who took part in all the events in May in Paris. At first, he went just to watch. I have known him since he was a small child. In the space of a month he has acquired an astonishing maturity. His intellectual honesty is rare. One of the first things he said upon arriving in Taizé was: "During this last month I had no way of knowing when I was pretending and when I was being authentic. I was searching. After having been beaten up, but especially seeing others mishandled, including girls, our solidarity went without saying; we didn't even have to think about it."

I particularly recall these words from our second conversation: "The really great difficulty is understanding what motivates the other person, understanding one another as human beings, going beyond one's own mental framework."

How does he remain so serene after what he experienced? Young people of that mettle are demanding. Until now, the young have been put too much to one side. Either we will build a new society all together, or there will be a split between two parallel societies. And all that will be left to us, the elderly, will be to look forward to a lonely death, in boredom and the affluence of consumer societies.

Anyone who wants to repress human dignity and spontaneity in a society or a group exposes that society or group to rebellion and its aftermath.

June 1968

More than three hours spent talking with a revolutionary student. He advocates a society of justice, arising out of human spontaneity. He accords full value to utopia as a creative force. But at the same time, he affirms bluntly that the assassination of Martin Luther King was a good thing. This act has liberated new energies. For him, King kept human beings from being liberated; he channeled the explosion of violence. Without him, the summer may turn out to be hot, destruction will be possible and that will matter in Europe.

I listen to him. His words cause something in me to bleed. At the same time I question myself. I ask myself what my own inconsistencies are and my unsuspected sectarian attitudes, when I see the person I am talking with manifest such obvious ones without realizing it.

June 1968

I have never prepared so much for a June 29. On this day[7] many priests are ordained. Some of them are friends. They are beginning their ministry at a very young age. They will have to face a society that is not interested in their commitment. They will no longer have, in the church, the protection of a whole people, the solid support of an earlier age. They will experience the ebb and flow of the years, discouragement, weariness, shining hopes abandoned.

Holiness is the only thing that will be able to open a way forward for them in the course of a long life. Without it, they will withdraw into themselves or look for compensations of all sorts. It alone will link them directly to Christ and to all the witnesses to the faith.

The provincial of a religious congregation has just spent two days here. He was on his way back from Niger, where he had lived close to a fraternity of Taizé brothers. He said to one of my brothers, a graduate of a technical institute who was working as a mason on a building site, "By your work you are taking part in human development." He was struck by the brother's reply: "Those around us do not know what a Christian is. We have to live first and foremost the holiness of Christ. Everything else, participating in development, will necessarily follow from this."

July 1968

When I saw our church built of concrete take shape, I entered a difficult period. Years later, I do not accept it that much more

7. The feast of Saints Peter and Paul.

easily; I would like it to be almost completely buried underground, scarcely visible to the eyes. Until now, we have all built things with certain norms of the non-provisional. But the mobility of the modern age leads us to imagine a church living as it were in tents.

This winter we destroyed the fixed elements inside our church. Concrete has not stopped us from achieving a flexible and mobile arrangement. The outside remains. What can we do? Surround it with trees? This whole experience taught us a lot. Concrete brings with it rigidity and the impression of strength.

July 1968

A group of forty young people asks me questions. The voice of a girl, pure and shy, hardly audible, asks me: with the little knowledge we possess, how can we manage to understand a contemporary world which is so complex?

My answer: to every woman, to every man, whatever may be the level of their knowledge, a living word is granted, sometimes just one. Putting it into practice disposes us to grasp from within the different trends of today.

This word brings us close to everyone, attentive to the peoples of China, Cuba, Eastern Europe, the United States, to prepare crossroads where one day those who are presently far apart will meet.

Back in my room, I continue the conversation with myself.

Human beings are created for hope. For them, all things become new. One day, at the heart of our darkness, a living word sheds light. That is what makes us open to others, irresistibly.

Christ does not force us to join him. The Gospel is not a vise to confine the consciences of other people and our own, as in a system. It is communion.

In Christ, God became poor, hidden. The sign of God cannot be an image of grandiosity. God does not ask us to accomplish great things too wonderful for us.[8] He simply wants us to understand how to love our brothers and sisters.

In these years a new birth can be glimpsed: God's people on the road towards a communion.

Prophecy is not dead. On the other side of the present violence, a young hope is arising.

Summer 1968

A member of a religious community asks me why, at Taizé, so many young people enter so intensely into the prayer. I tell him that, in the last few days, a surprising experience occurred on two different occasions. A group of young people attended the prayer for the first time and then left. The next day, they came back and stayed for a few days, days they had set aside to go to the seaside.

Another group had exactly the same experience a week later, although there was no contact between the two groups. A few hours after leaving, there they were again, to stay for a few days.

I asked them why. Their reply: they were looking for God. For them, the most essential thing here was the communal prayer. Why? Because it is carried forward each day by men in whom they sense a commitment.

In addition, is not communal prayer a place where time takes on a different character, where it acquires a weight of eternity? Through the prayer of the church, all together we are provisionally released from the grip of time. That is what counts for people today, harassed by the demands of a civilization of profit and technology.

Could praying with so many young people make us tend to forget adults? Nothing could be further from the truth. Anyone who has known how to listen to elderly people has often received a treasure. And when, at certain periods of the year, children pray alongside us, another sign of complementarity is given. All the generations together bear a living word.

8. Ps 131:1.

Here as elsewhere, reciprocity counts. If a community such as ours perseveres day after day, it owes this to the faithfulness of so many women, men, and children. They are present here, and they sustain us.

Recently, some parents were here with five of their children. Since they were not French-speakers, they could not understand a word. The regular attendance of the children at prayer preoccupied the parents. They felt, in all honesty, that they ought to put an end to it. The children replied: you can go on holiday elsewhere; we are staying here. Beyond an understanding of the words, something more essential had got across.

1968

This evening some young people asked me about the meaning of *gratuité*.[9] It is the act of a person who refuses to keep another person captive. This act involves a crossing, a passover. Trampling oneself underfoot, one could say using heroic language. This passover leads to a communion. When it occurs, it opens up to life, incomparably.

1968?

This evening, on television, there was a program with a bishop and some lay people. The harshness of one of them led to a feeling of uneasiness.

The bitterness of some people, their revolt, are not pleasant to see. The bishop, a shy man, came off well by contrast, although it is true that his replies could have been more welcoming.

---

9. A French word difficult to translate. "Gratuitousness" has a more trivial or even negative connotation in English. One could also say "having no ulterior motives, being selfless, disinterested (not to be confused with uninterested)."

1968

How many times have I appealed to the unity of the personality! What I meant by that was the reconciliation of ourselves with God. But I have become aware of the daily combat this requires, regardless of age. I see the discontinuities, the roads not taken. In the end I wonder whether the unity of the personality is not too pretentious a goal.

It is granted momentarily but, to be honest with myself, I have to recognize that it does not represent a state I have attained or in which I remain. It is a direction to which one has to return constantly. This effort must be begun over and over again. Harmonizing opposites so they are transformed into complementarities.

If Paul had not written to the Thessalonians that their faith was making great progress[10] I would be inclined to think that no one can hope for an upward journey. On the other hand, when he adds that their love for others is growing, that I can easily understand. The more we advance, the more sensitive we become to others. Anyone who suffers because of themselves can acquire an exceptional ability to understand every human situation!

But does our faith progress as well? Does it become easier when, over the course of many years, it has been confirmed by repeated signs? There remain many situations when it is at a loss.

Similarly, there are situations we are unable to leave behind and move on. In 1962, to contribute to the formation of a cooperative, we donated our herd of cows, which we had patiently selected over the years.[11] Giving up some possessions was a relief.

But in the long run, the absence of farm animals has made itself felt. Life in the countryside loses part of its meaning for those who no longer take part intensely in farming. Nothing enabled us better to follow the cycle of the seasons than that herd.

That splendid moment of milking the cows, repeated morning and evening, was no more. In the early years, I was the only one to do the milking every day. No more calves being born. Helping

10. 2 Thess 1:3.
11. See note 8, p. 53.

the mother to give birth does not leave you indifferent and even possesses a certain gravity. The years have passed since our cows have joined the collective farm. Creating that was a joy, but it has not filled the void of a full barn next to our house.

1968

If we affirm that there are depths in human beings of which we can know almost nothing, are we playing into the hands of psychoanalysis? I am not well acquainted with that science, but I remain marked by a conversation I had with a great authority on psychoanalysis.[12]

For him, far from being a cure-all, it ought to be humble in its conclusions. It sometimes happens that, after an analysis, it is unable to reach a synthesis. An inner anarchy has only increased in the process.

In his opinion, if every human being is affected by neurotic elements, what matters in the end is making good use of sicknesses or neurotic states. If they do not foster creativity but are on the contrary destructive, then medical help is a good thing. Psychoanalysis remains a remedy which it is beneficial to employ when no others are effective.

He reminded me that the age-old practice of intuition, known as "spiritual direction," has always been effective in the church. It too is capable of discerning in people the inner fissures into which the very bases of the personality collapse and which lead to serious imbalances. And such imbalances do not allow people in the vicinity to escape unscathed. In the long run they can contaminate.

He spoke to me of some doctors, deeply afflicted themselves, who became psychoanalysts without undergoing afterwards the regular checkups that are necessary. Very quickly they become great gurus of the present century. They claim to have the key

12. Peter Rutishauser, a psychoanalyst from Zurich who came to Taizé in 1968 for a silent retreat. Deeply impressed by his outlook, Brother Roger continued the relationship and encouraged several brothers to speak with him until his death in 1972.

to knowledge, whereas they bring only failures and ruin in their wake.

The modesty of this physician inspired full confidence in analysis seriously applied. In him, it had become neither a system nor a philosophy.

1968?

In every community, rifts and splits, of whatever sort, are a sign of sectarianism.

Why does segregation always keep infiltrating the church of God? In the past older people tended to exclude the young. Today things are starting to head in the other direction. It hurts to hear people disparage old women who are believers.

In this respect, some words spoken by the grandmother of one of my brothers comes to mind: "I never get bored, since He is always present." And she showed an image of Christ on the road to Emmaus.

I never get bored. I heard my own mother say those same words.

They will never cease to astonish us, those women advanced in years who, by their courage and the power of their dedication, motivate those who are younger.

SELECT BIBLIOGRAPHY

Writings by Brother Roger

Fidanzio, Marcello, ed. *Brother Roger of Taizé: Essential Writings*. Maryknoll, NY: Orbis, 2006.
Anthology with biographical introduction.

Dynamic of the Provisional. London: Mowbray, 1981.

Glimmers of Happiness. Chicago: GIA, 2007.
Brother Roger reflects on events and people that influenced his life and calling.

God is Love Alone. Chicago: GIA, 2003.
The essentials of Brother Roger's thinking and personal accounts from the story of Taizé.

Peace of Heart in All Things. Chicago: GIA, 2004.
A brief meditation for each day of the year.

The Rule of Taizé. London: SPCK, 2013.
The original text expressing the fundamentals of the life of the Taizé Community.

Books about Taizé

Clément, Olivier. *Taizé: A Meaning to Life*. Chicago: GIA, 1997.
Santos, Jason Brian. *A Community Called Taizé: A Story of Prayer, Worship and Reconciliation*. Downers Grove, IL: IVP, 2008.
Spink, Kathryn. *A Universal Heart:The Life and Vision of Brother Roger of Taizé*. Chicago: GIA, 1986, 2005.

DVDs (available at www.giamusic.com)

Moments in the Life of Brother Roger
Meeting Brother Roger of Taizé

www.taize.fr

Information in 28 languages about the community, meetings at Taizé and elsewhere (online registration), suggestions for prayer, the songs of Taizé etc.

Subject Index